# When They Don't All Speak English

# When They Don't All Speak English

## Integrating the ESL Student into the Regular Classroom

Edited by

**Pat Rigg**
American Language and Literacy, Tucson

**Virginia G. Allen**
The Ohio State University

National Council of Teachers of English
1111 Kenyon Road, Urbana, Illinois 61801

Staff Editor: Michelle Sanden Johlas

Cover Design: Michael J. Getz

Cover Photograph: Brad May, Mount Lebanon School District, Pittsburgh

Interior Design: Tom Kovacs for TGK Design

NCTE Stock Number 56932-3020

**Library of Congress Cataloging-in-Publication Data**
When they don't all speak English : integrating the ESL student into
   the regular classroom / edited by Pat Rigg, Virginia G. Allen.
      p.     cm.
   Bibliography: p.
   ISBN 0-8141-5693-2
   1. English language—Study and teaching—Foreign speakers.
I. Rigg, Pat.   II. Allen, Virginia Garibaldi.
PE1128.W714   1989
428'.007—dc20                                                    89-35552
                                                                    CIP

# Contents

# Introduction

It is now very likely that regular classroom teachers will work
with language-different children. According to the latest census
figures more than eight million school-aged children live in
homes in which languages other than English are spoken. The
continuing arrival of large groups of refugees makes it more
and more probable that the classroom teacher will be asked to
teach children who do not yet speak English (Allen 1986).

The international organization of Teachers of English to Speakers of
Other Languages (TESOL) estimates that every classroom teacher at
some time during his or her career will have at least one student
who speaks English as another language. This book is written for
these teachers. Almost none of these teachers have received any
formal training in teaching English as another language, and almost
all must rely on their own good sense, their sensitivity to their
students—whatever languages they speak—and their ability as professionals to alter the curriculum to suit their students, selecting the
materials and techniques which best fit. Sometimes there are work-
shops that address some of the problems these teachers face, either
in their district or at conventions, but for the most part they go it
alone. They do their best, but they do it without adequate information
from professional language teachers—especially information on how
to integrate new speakers of English into their class. This book offers
that information.

## Principles That Make for Good Practice

In this introduction we offer the principles that we feel are the most
important for teachers to know about language learners and language
learning, and we discuss in a general way the applications of those
principles to classrooms, K–12. Following this is an overview of the
volume, with brief summaries of the chapters. Finally, we offer a
brief bibliography of suggestions for further reading.

*Principles*

1. People who are learning another language are, first of all, people.
2. Learning a language means learning to do the things you want to do with people who speak that language.
3. A person's second language, like the first, develops globally, not linearly.
4. Language develops best in a variety of rich contexts.
5. Literacy is part of language, so writing and reading develop alongside speaking and listening.

Let's look more deeply at each of these in turn.

*Principles into Practice*

*Principle 1.* It seems so obvious that people who are learning another language are, first of all, people, that one wonders why it needs to be said at all. We list this principle first because it is the most important and, although it is obvious, it seems frequently forgotten. We have seen many students placed two, three, or more years behind their age-mates because they do not speak English, as though speaking a language other than English were a terrible form of retardation that prevented the children from communicating with and playing with other children their own age. It is harder to be an eleven-year-old in a second grade class than to be an eleven-year-old in a fifth grade class, even if the second grade curriculum looks easier.

Children who are learning another language are, first of all, children. They have the same needs as other children their age. Like all children, they need to feel good about themselves and about their relationships to those around them. They need opportunities to be successful in school, and if their English is not proficient enough for them to be successful with academic assignments, the teacher can find nonacademic opportunities for success. They need plenty of opportunities, in class as well as outside it, to form friendships and to do things with their friends. Children's developmental stages are more important than levels of English proficiency. In addition, children's cognitive development proceeds similarly across cultures, so second-language children are ready to explore the same concepts that their age group is exploring.

The principle that people learning another language are, first, people, applies to older language learners as much as it does to children. It is just as important, perhaps even more important, for teenagers to be with their own age group as it is for younger students.

Students learning English as another language already have command of a language and a culture that, usually, neither the teacher nor the other students have. They are not deficient or limited in any way; rather, they can be a rich source of information and assistance in teaching many things, from social studies to values clarification.

The clearest application of this first principle to school organization is this: second-language students need to be with first-language students. If they are isolated from native-English-speaking students, they cannot learn English from them, nor can they share any of the riches they have to offer. Classrooms should be organized so that small groups of first-language and second-language students work together on meaningful tasks.

In emphasizing the similarities among children, we don't want to overlook individual differences. Refugee children may have traumatic histories and thus require more emotional support than some other children. Many Southeast Asian children have watched friends and family members die horribly; their journey to North America has been an act of courage and endurance that few of us born here will ever be asked to match. Often they cannot talk about the horrors they have experienced, for psychological as well as for linguistic reasons. Many teachers, especially those in elementary schools, are sensitive to their students' moods; that sensitivity and delicacy are a teacher's greatest assets when working with students who have suffered traumas. Sensitive teachers recognize the individuality of each student; they don't lump all of their students together. That is important with students learning English, too: there are enormous differences in the backgrounds of a Hmong villager and a Vietnamese doctor, for example, and added to these differences are differences in life history, in present situation, and in individual temperament, talents, and interests. Urzúa's "A Children's Story" (1986) discusses many factors in the school and home that can affect second-language learners.

*Principle 2.* Learning a language means learning to do the things you want to do with people who speak that language. It doesn't mean learning forms of language to use someday in some possible situation: it means using the language (however badly) today, now, to do things. We can contrast the typical dialogue given in a foreign language class with dialogue overheard on a playground.

| Foreign Language Dialogue (translated) | Dialogue Overheard on a Playground |
|---|---|
| *A:* Hello, Isabel. How are you? | *A:* Want to play? |

*B:* Fine, thanks. And you?              *B:* OK.

The foreign language dialogue practices forms for future use, for the day one will actually be able to greet someone; the overheard dialogue is what two children actually said, the forms they used in order to start playing together. The meaning of the invitation to play was clear from the context: one girl with a ball held it out to another, established eye contact, and raised her brows as she spoke. The other child did not need to say anything, certainly not "in complete sentences"; she needed only to return the eye contact, smile slightly, and walk forward to the ball with one hand out. She said, "OK," indicating that she had mastered one of America's great contributions to English. The formula *OK* can be used in a great variety of situations: with rising intonation it becomes a question, with emphatic intonation it becomes an expression of strong agreement and solidarity. Some visitors to the United States have suggested that it is possible to cross the country using only that phrase.

The child who said "OK" had a chance to hear authentic language in a context that, in a sense, taught the language appropriate to that context. It is not as appropriate for one child on a playground to say to another, "Hello, how are you?" as to say, "Wanna play?" Children on the playground teach the ESL child the language by playing. They develop their own ways of communicating, ways the teacher may not be aware of, but ways that are effective at making meaning together. ESL speakers need many, many chances to use the language in a wide variety of situations like the playground, where the emphasis is on using English to do what they want to do, not on producing correct forms of the language. Classrooms should be organized so that small groups of first-language and second-language students work together on meaningful tasks that nudge children to use language, so that the same sort of communication and teaching that happens on the playground can happen inside the classroom.

Language development means learning to use a language to socialize, to learn, to query, to make believe, and to wonder. All of that takes many years to learn, whether it is the first language or the second. Many teachers have students in their classes who have had two years of ESL training and who now are placed in all-English environments and expected to perform as well as their classmates. Some do, but the majority struggle. How many of us could carry a full academic load in a new country with only two years' training in that language? Second-language students need continuing but changing kinds of support as they develop English. That support should not be stopped after one, two, or three years, but should be modified in ways to help the learner develop the kind of language needed for academic success. Some schools offer pull-out classes; for part of each day ESL students meet with a teacher of English as a second language. These classes permit students to receive the focused attention of an adult trained in second-language development; such classes can be invaluable sources of information for the regular classroom teacher, because the teacher of English as a second language, or TESL, is best qualified to determine the ESL student's progress in English and to make suggestions to the classroom teacher. While such classes provide invaluable assistance, they are not sufficient. The regular classroom teacher also needs to adjust the classroom so that the second-language student can proceed to learn both the language and the content subjects as fast as possible.

*Principle 3.* A person's second language, like the first, develops globally, not linearly. Language is not learned as a jigsaw of tiny bits of mastered skills, each fitting into a pattern, but rather as an entire picture that is at first blurred, only gradually coming into focus. Anyone who has watched a one-year-old child becoming a language user has seen this: the toddler's pronunciation, vocabulary, and grammar are so inadequate that the baby's initial attempts at communication cannot be understood without a caregiver who, knowing the context, focuses on possible meanings, not on eliciting some adult standard of speech from the child. As the toddler's understanding of the world enlarges, so does the child's language: a three-year-old can talk about a number of things, but pronunciation, vocabulary, and grammar, although noticeably better than two years earlier, still are far from an adult standard. (See Wells 1986, for a clear, research-based discussion of first-language development.) Second-language development is not identical to first-language development, but in this important respect it is: it develops globally, not piecemeal.

What does this mean to the classroom teacher? It means, first, that we should offer our second-language students a rich bath of language, not a string of language beads, one bead at a time. We should not waste the students' time with worksheets, word lists, or pronunciation drills; these are little pieces of a jigsaw that the student is expected to fit together without having seen the picture of the completed puzzle. Instead, we should make sure that our second-language students are constantly engaged in meaningful activities with their first-language classmates, activities in which the students talk with each other. Most of these activities concern academic tasks. (See Rigg and Enright's "Endnote" [1986] for an example of one teacher's classroom.) For example, if a first grade teacher is attempting to teach concepts of measurement and distance, the children can use tape measures or lengths of string to measure how far each can hop, or how long a giant step is in the game "Mother, May I," and in small groups record their measurements, deciding which was the smallest and longest, and then the groups can share and compare with the entire class. A junior high teacher working with more sophisticated sorts of students and measurements can have small groups of two or three students design and fly paper airplanes. The students use measurements in the design and production of their airplanes and in determining flight distances. If they take an average of three flights, they also are using some numerical skills. They can make a class chart of time in flight and flight distance.

When the class is arranged so that the students work together to pose and to solve problems, students will talk with each other about the problem and solutions. That talk is the "warm bath of language" that we referred to earlier; the second-language learner hears and participates in conversation that is usually meaningful because the context makes the meaning clear. Of course, when students are working with concrete items that they can manipulate, it's much easier for the beginning ESL speaker to comprehend. If a group is solving the problem of what sort of plane flies farthest, it is easier for a second-language student to comprehend what's going on than if the group is discussing an issue of student government. For this reason, science and art curricula offer many opportunities for groups to work with concrete items and for the ESL student to learn more English by working with the group. These content areas are not the only ones that offer possibilities for group problem solving: the airplane contest fits into the math curriculum. In social studies, groups of students studying communities can make models of buildings, which offers opportunities to form, shape, build, and to talk about all of these. This all relates directly to the fourth principle.

*Principle 4.* Language develops best in a variety of rich contexts. Ideal situations are those in which the student understands what's happening and is also learning something new. Materials can be part of rich contexts: for example, children manipulating magnets and iron filings develop new concepts and the vocabulary to talk about those concepts. Whenever possible the class should leave the classroom, because the community outside offers so many potentially rich contexts for all of the students to learn from. A field trip does not necessarily need a school bus, parental permission slips, and sack lunches: a walk around the block just outside the school can offer innumerable opportunities for considering questions that fascinate students. For example, how much debris is there in this one-meter square? Is there more in that one than in another square meter? What, exactly, forms the debris? What does this suggest about the people who have passed by? These are the same questions an archaeologist asks; young students can ask the same, and can use the same basic archaeological techniques and logic to address these questions. Most schools have parking lots; a trip to the lot offers the same sorts of opportunities as a walk round the school. What sorts of cars are parked there, with specifics of brands, years, countries of origin? What are the physical characteristics of the cars and motorcycles, their composition, color, weight, etc.? Do the schools in the ESL students' countries also have parking lots? What similarities and differences are there in how people get to school? Students themselves can think of many more questions, questions that they themselves find interesting. These are just two suggestions for using the school grounds. Trips that go further afield are certainly recommended. It is important to note that it is not the location or materials that make the context: it is what the students do at the location or with the materials. If they are working together on a topic of mutual interest with plenty of opportunity for conversation, both first- and second-language students benefit. This applies to printed material just as it does to concrete items. A book that has clear illustrations of the text may be readable for a second-language student, if the student is working with a classmate, and the two have chances to discuss the book, comparing their impressions and reactions.

*Principle 5.* Literacy is part of language development. Writing, speaking, listening, and reading all nourish one another; we don't wait for mastery of one before encouraging development of the other three. This principle applied to classroom organization means that ESL speakers should be involved with literacy activities from the first. Second-language students should not be expected to keep up with a class reading group, but they should also not be refused the chance to read. They need not be fluent English speakers before they can write and read.

They need to hear literature read aloud by the teacher, because this is one of the easiest ways (and one of the most enjoyable for the entire class) for the second-language student to discover the sorts of English that we call "literary." This is how they learn the structure of narratives in English; it's how they learn "once upon a time," "happily ever after," and many other phrases. More, they learn the sorts of English that are found only in literature, and their reading, writing, and conversation are all enriched by this.

They need to have reading materials that are comprehensible. Often, it is quite difficult for a teacher to select such materials: materials mandated by the curriculum, such as basals, may be difficult for all the students to read, especially if the books are written to readability formulas rather than to high standards of children's literature. These are almost impossible to read for a student who is just beginning to know the second language. ESL students sometimes appear to understand skill exercises from reading workbooks and dutifully underline where they're told, but these exercises almost always fragment language, and therefore are not reading material, but just a meaningless ritual. For the student who is just beginning literacy in English, the language experience approach offers a technique for producing individual reading materials for the ESL students, because those materials reflect the students' ideas phrased in their ways. Picture books with strong illustrations and stories with predictable patterns and repetitive language can help children comprehend text. (See the individual chapters by Rigg and by Allen in this volume for more specific information on these techniques.)

Even students just beginning to learn English can write, as long as the writing is authentic; that is, it is the student's own composition for the student's own purposes, not a product for the teacher's evaluation. Even if a child can only make a couple of marks on a drawing to indicate ownership, that is authentic writing. Careful copying of a set of sentences from the board, however much it looks like English, is not authentic writing. Students with a little English proficiency can keep dialogue journals, which they can share with the teacher every other week or so; the teacher replies in the journal, commenting only on the content, never on the forms of language used. Other sorts of authentic writing that occur naturally in active classrooms include keeping records of the care given the class gerbil, fish, or other animals; keeping records of other classroom chores, a kind of "K.P." list; charting all sorts of information, from the number of blocks each student travels from home, to seconds of flight time with the paper airplanes; writing a script for a play, perhaps based on a story the teacher has read to the class; writing the rules for a game that one group makes for another; and more. Obviously, many of these can be best done in small groups. Every writing activity suggested here is closely integrated with conversation and with reading; those aspects of language both inform and are informed by the students' writing.

When all of the principles that we've listed are put into practice, a meaning-centered classroom emerges, one in which the curriculum is set more by the teacher than by some central committee that has never met these particular students. The students work in small groups much of the time—second-language students integrated with first-language students—on projects that the students believe are relevant to them. A classroom that is meaning-centered doesn't waste time on meaningless pursuits, and the amount of time saved by omitting meaningless exercises is enormous. There is ample time for daily sustained silent reading, for daily journal writing, for teacher-read stories, and for whole-class sharing of individual and group project updates. This kind of classroom makes for the best language development for students using English as their native tongue and for students who are using English as another tongue. We like to call them **REAL** students: **R**eaders and writers of **E**nglish as **A**nother **L**anguage.

## Overview of Chapters

Before we summarize the individual chapters, we want to indicate how each one relates to the whole. The first chapter, by Jean Handscombe, describes the variety of students in ESL programs and lists the characteristics of a quality program for them. Next, Carole Urzúa spells out what the classroom language arts teacher and the ESL teacher can learn from each other. The next four chapters focus on elementary students: Judith Wells Lindfors points out the characteristics of a quality elementary classroom; Virginia G. Allen describes the contributions that literature can make to REAL students; Pat Rigg tells why and how to use the language experience approach; and Elizabeth A. Franklin's careful, detailed study of one youngster's art and writing indicates how observation can inform teaching. Carole Edelsky speaks to upper elementary and secondary teachers as she explains how to use language variation in the school's surrounding community as a strength—a subject of study as well as a means of learning. The next two chapters focus on secondary students: Anna Uhl Chamot and J. Michael O'Malley present their CALLA model, its theoretical foundation, and its in-school application; David Freeman and Yvonne S. Freeman report on a summer school program that may be a model for districts wishing to prevent dropouts and pushouts. In the final chapter, Sarah Hudelson indicates how teachers—whether elementary, middle, or secondary—can incorporate English into content areas, so that they teach the language at the same time that they are fulfilling curriculum objectives.

*A Quality Program*

As a New Canadian, Jean Handscombe understands firsthand many of the issues facing immigrants to this continent. Her chapter addresses the questions: Who are these students? What sorts of support do they need? How can we best get that support to them? In answering these questions, she relies on the programs she has helped to develop in Ontario, programs that are international models. The Canadian government and the provincial governments within Canada have accepted the responsibility, financial as well as ethical, for integrating New Canadians. They recognize that allowing immigrants and refugees to enter their borders commits the governments to support the newcomers in their attempts to become full-fledged citizens, with all that that means in terms of learning English, gaining employment suitable to their education and experience, obtaining decent housing and health care, and so on. Both federal and state governments in the United States of America could improve their programs a great deal by emulating the Canadians.

Handscombe reminds us that there are widely varying groups of students for whom English is another language: immigrants, refugees, international students, and second-generation immigrants, not to mention those people whose language and cultures on this continent antedate any English speakers—native peoples and speakers of French and Spanish. Handscombe lists three factors to consider in placing and teaching these different students: their educational backgrounds, which can differ dramatically; the proficiency level of English that they require; and whether the school demonstrates that it values these students' home cultures. She then outlines the sorts of support these students need, describing five key components of a quality program: orientation, monitoring, parental involvement, language, and academic upgrading.

*I Grow for a Living*

Carole Urzúa's chapter brings together applications of current and recent research in both first- and second-language development. She notes the knowledge gap between two groups—mainstream teachers, who know a lot about language arts, and ESL teachers, who know a lot about second-language development. Each group has remained relatively ignorant of what the other group knows. Urzúa seeks to bridge that gap. She summarizes insights from recent research in reading and composition—from such scholars as the Goodmans in reading, and Atwell, Calkins, and Graves in writing. Urzúa explains how those insights translate into classroom practice, especially when the students are Readers and writers of English as Another Language. She also summarizes findings of recent research from such linguistic scholars as Krashen and indicates how those findings translate into practice in the regular classroom in which a few students are REAL.

## The Classroom: A Good Environment for Language Learning

Judith Wells Lindfors asks of any classroom material or activity, "Would this make sense outside the classroom?" and this touchstone is one which her graduate and undergraduate students quickly adopt, focusing their classes on meaning rather than on form.

In this chapter, Lindfors first notes how all children develop their first language with little observable effort, and she asserts that the two major factors responsible are (1) the environment, and (2) the ways a young language learner uses the environment. Then she applies her touchstone to a classroom in which authentic interaction can take place among the students, and she indicates how three rather standard language arts activities—show and tell, reading stories, and writing dialogue journals—help this interaction at the same time that they help the REAL students develop English.

## Literature as a Support to Language Acquisition

Virginia G. Allen's chapter asserts that children's literature offers a great deal to the REAL student (as well as to the native speaker of English). This is not literature rewritten to some "readability" formula that restricts vocabulary and syntax. As Rigg (1986) points out, such formulas are "a house of cards." In *Report Card on Basal Readers* (1988), K. Goodman and others show why reading materials that are rewritten to formulas are less readable than the originals. Allen here refers to such classics as *The Gingerbread Man, Three Little Pigs*, and *The Little Red Hen*, as well as to modern children's literature such as Hutchins's *Titch*, de Paolo's *Strega Nona*, and the Woods' *Napping House*. Observing and reporting on one REAL student as an example, Allen shows that even a student who doesn't speak in class can understand and enjoy a good story such as *The Gingerbread Man*. The student can talk about the story afterwards, because the language with which to discuss the story comes from the story itself. Allen says that in selecting works of literature, teachers need to look for predictability in plot line, in repetitive language, and in illustrations that help comprehension; they also need to choose books that can be incorporated into students' further learning through writing and collaborative conversations. Hough, Nuss, and Enright (1986) agree, and suggest specific ways the teacher who is reading aloud can increase students' comprehension.

### Language Experience Approach: Reading Naturally

Pat Rigg describes how the language experience approach (LEA) can be used to elicit reading material for the REAL student who is just becoming literate, regardless of the student's age. She explains why teachers need to accept, without correction, each student's contribution to the story, however ungrammatical. Rigg indicates how this approach moves from students dictating into students writing for themselves.

### Encouraging and Understanding Visual and Written Works

Elizabeth A. Franklin's chapter builds on the work of Patricia Carini, who has for years advocated learning from students. Franklin looks in great detail at the art and writing of one student, demonstrating with this one little girl how much observant teachers can learn about their students. Elementary teachers may want to copy Franklin's ideas, setting up conditions so that students will draw, paint, write, and dictate, and then studying these products to learn more about each student, adding observation notes of the contexts.

### Putting Language Variation to Work

Carole Edelsky's chapter, like Sarah Hudelson's later in this volume, addresses the question of how to combine academic activities with language teaching so that the students gain in both areas. Edelsky suggests having the students act as budding linguists, studying the variation in language use in their own homes and their own communities, and she details just how this can be done.

### The Cognitive Academic Language Learning Approach

Anna Uhl Chamot and J. Michael O'Malley speak to the often-forgotten secondary school teacher who sees each student for less than an hour a day, but is expected to keep all students up with the assigned curriculum, even the ESL student who can't read the textbook, much less write answers to the questions following the chapters. Chamot and O'Malley have developed an approach to this problem, named CALLA, the Cognitive Academic Language Learning Approach, which offers guidelines for helping the ESL student ease into the mainstream. Beginning with a brief outline of their theoretical foundation, Chamot and O'Malley present the principles of CALLA and then suggest how these principles might be applied to a lesson.

## A Road to Success

David Freeman and Yvonne S. Freeman report on a summer program with at-risk Hispanic and Yaqui secondary students. Using four principles of teaching and learning, the teachers worked with these students to help them succeed in two courses required for gradua-tion—biology and United States history. The summer program was significant not only because the students developed academically, but also because they gained confidence in themselves and in their academic abilities.

## "Teaching" English through Content-area Activities

Sarah Hudelson points out that as students whose native language is not English enter our schools in ever increasing numbers, a major responsibility of the schools has become both to facilitate students' ability to use English to accomplish their own aims or purposes and to use English to achieve in school, to use English to learn school content (e.g., math, science, social studies, etc.) This chapter details one way in which elementary and secondary teachers may use content-area objectives and develop units of activities based on content and on current information available about second-language development. The chapter includes examples of content-area objectives and activities for a variety of age levels.

Pat Rigg and Virginia G. Allen

## References

Allen, V. G. 1986. Developing Contexts to Support Second Language Acquisition. *Language Arts* 63:61–66.

Goodman, K. S., et al. 1988. *Report Card on Basal Readers*. New York: Richard C. Owen.

Hough, R., J. R. Nuss, and D. S. Enright. 1986. Story Reading with Limited English Speaking Children in the Regular Classroom. *TESL Canada Journal* 3 (2): 510–14.

Rigg, P. 1986. Reading in ESL: Learning from Kids. In *Children and ESL: Integrating Perspectives*, edited by P. Rigg and D. S. Enright. Washington, D.C.: TESOL.

Rigg, P., and D. S. Enright. 1986. *Children and ESL: Integrating Perspectives.* Washington, D.C.: TESOL.

Urzúa, C. 1986. A Children's Story. In *Children and ESL: Integrating Perspectives*, edited by P. Rigg and D. S. Enright. Washington, D.C.: TESOL.

Wells, G. 1986. *The Meaning Makers.* Portsmouth, N.H.: Heinemann.

## Suggestions for Further Reading

Enright, D. S., and M. L. McCloskey. 1985. Yes, Talking! Organizing the Classroom to Promote Second Language Acquisition. *TESOL Quarterly* 19 (3): 431–53.

———. 1988. *Integrating English.* Reading, Mass.: Addison-Wesley.

Hudelson, S. 1984. Kan Yu Ret an Rayt en Ingles: Children Become Literate in English as a Second Language. *TESOL Quarterly* 18:221–38.

Rigg, P., and S. Hudelson. 1986. One Child Doesn't Speak English. *Australian Journal of Reading* 9 (3): 116–25.

# 1 A Quality Program for Learners of English as a Second Language

Jean Handscombe
North York Board of Education, Toronto

## Who Are These Students?

The classrooms of North American schools contain many children who have a need to add a good command of English to their fluency in the language which they have learned and used before coming to school (Ashworth 1988; Oxford et al. 1981).*

The children learning English as a second language with the longest history of living in these parts of the world belong to North American Indian and Inuit families. This article, focusing as it does on the needs of first- and second-generation immigrant and refugee students and temporary residents, does not address itself to the topic of quality education for native peoples. However, many of the suggestions for programming included here owe much to the history—both positive and negative—of native people's schooling.

Even with this narrower focus on more recent arrivals, these students constitute a highly heterogeneous group. Their family background variables, as listed by Ovando and Collier (1985) include dimensions such as immigrant or native-born; reasons for emigration; length of residency in North America; existence of relatives in the home country and the frequency of visits back there; rural versus urban tradition; socioeconomic profile; position and responsibilities within the family; nature of students' and parents' previous academic

---

* To borrow Lawrence Carrington's phrase, certain terms are used in this article as "convenient inexactitudes" (Carrington 1983). *Second* in "second-language learners" may, in fact, refer to the second but also to the third, fourth, or *n*th language which the student is learning. *Language* is used to refer both to what people usually refer to as languages, e.g., Spanish, Korean, Punjabi, and English, but here also includes Creoles. Creoles develop as a result of contact between groups of people who have no language in common and need a compromise medium of communication. Despite the English lexical base of many of the Creoles now heard in North American settings, their semantics, grammar, and phonology are sufficiently different from English to classify them as languages rather than as dialects.

1

experiences; parents' aspirations for themselves and their children; and parents' expectations of the school. Among the recent arrivals, four major subgroups can be identified.

## Immigrants

These students usually arrive in their new country accompanied by at least one parent, though in the case of children from the Caribbean, for example, they may be coming to join their parent(s) after a considerable period of separation. Most have been to school in their country of origin, with the quality of that schooling ranging from excellent to very poor. Often the children had little input into the decision to emigrate and their attitude on arrival may be one of apprehension and resistance, since they still identify emotionally with the people and places they have left behind. Both children and adults go through various stages of adjustment during their first few years in a new country, and family stress is to be expected, particularly as the wage-earners try to establish themselves within the workforce. For many children, their arrival in North America also provides their first experience of being a member of a racial or ethnic minority.

## Refugees

Wherever there has been serious political conflict in the world, individuals and groups who fear for their lives or who know they will not be allowed to live as citizens with rights equal to those of others within their own country have sought refuge in countries such as Canada and the United States. Their gratitude for having been granted a safe place to live is often tempered by the sense of loss they feel in having had to leave their homeland, family, and friends, with only the remotest possibility of ever returning. Refugees usually have had to leave behind most of their possessions, including records of employment and education. What they often bring, however, are vivid and painful memories of violence. Processing refugee claims frequently involves long delays, and many of the children now entering our schools have spent several years in another country, waiting for approval from government officials. Their schooling during that time usually consists of a few hours a week of lessons taught by a volunteer. These students often require substantial academic upgrading on arrival, as well as skilled and sensitive counseling to help them deal with the traumatic events of their recent lives.

## International Students

Both United States and Canadian schools each year welcome a number of students from overseas who come here to attend school on a student visa and pay for doing so, in addition to those who come on one of several bilateral student exchange programs or as the dependents of people who have been invited for specific short-term business or academic purposes. Those who come to buy an education in North America often do so largely because of the intense pressure in their own countries for places in top secondary schools and universities. Increasingly, students from Hong Kong, for example, are being sent by parents as the first step toward establishing the family in North America. For almost all of these fee-paying students, their arrival here marks their first separation from parents and their first experience of living away from a family unit. Though some come from wealthy families, others have parents and siblings who have made considerable personal sacrifices so that one child of the family may study abroad. Many of these students have attended schools where English is a major medium of instruction. Whereas their English may have seemed adequate within a bilingual setting, they soon realize that much higher levels of proficiency are required to be successful in North American schools and universities.

## Second-generation Immigrants

Immigration statistics often conceal the enormous numbers of children who, born in the United States or Canada, have been brought up as part of a family whose life is conducted in language(s) other than English and whose values and behaviors are influenced by the cultural group(s) with which their parents identify. When there is a mismatch between the language and culture of the school and the language and culture of the children, many of these students remain silent during their early days in school and show evidence of a different socialization from that which has been considered the norm. Many North American-born children entering our schools are used to hearing and using Creole, based lexically on English but differing substantially otherwise, and may not yet have become proficient in English. Their parents, many of whom can use both languages, recognize the richness and precision of their Creole and its effectiveness as a medium of communication and cultural transmission. At the same time, they are aware of the need for their children to become proficient in English because of its use in school, in public and professional life, and in the wider community (Carrington 1983).

## What Kind of Support Do They Need?

For many years the assumption has been that the source of difficulty for all these groups of students lay in their lack of familiarity with English. The labels used to describe them—non-English-speaking, limited English proficient—and the title given to the programs and teachers often provided to help them—English as a Second Language—underscore this assumption. It was thought that once students had learned English they no longer would be at a disadvantage and could be fully integrated into the work of the regular classroom. But experience, as well as research in the field of minority student education around the world (Brumfit et al. 1985; McGroarty 1986), has raised some questions as to the wisdom of putting so much faith in a single solution to such a complex problem. Though undoubtedly the development of proficiency in English is a prerequisite for success in a school system that uses English as its primary medium of instruction, other factors must also be taken into account.

### *Students Differ in Their Educational Backgrounds*

Over the past twenty years, we have learned a great deal about the interplay between learning concepts and learning language (Donaldson 1978; Lindfors 1987; Wells and Wells 1984). We have also begun to recognize the possibilities for transfer of skills between a student's first language and subsequent ones (Cummins 1984). Students with a well-developed conceptual framework and a high level of proficiency in the first language may be held back by an English-language teaching program designed for students who lack such background. Similarly, students who have had little schooling and whose proficiency in their first language is limited may be overwhelmed by a program of English-language instruction that takes for granted a more extensive conceptual and linguistic base. As an example, consider one child who knows how to tell time in his or her first language and one who does not. If both are in a second-language program which groups students by level of English-language proficiency and focuses only on the language to be learned, when it comes to a lesson on telling time, the child who already knows how to do it in the first language will probably learn the English equivalent and the other will not, at least not then. In short, a program for these students that does not also attend to their conceptual development is likely to produce very uneven patterns of English-language development and its resulting academic achievement.

### Students Require High Levels of English Proficiency

Linked to the issue of the relationship between linguistic and conceptual development is the question of the *amount* and *kind* of English that these students need to learn. All too often in the past, students have been demitted from special support programs because, having acquired a superficial oral fluency that enabled them to hold a simple conversation and to express their basic personal needs, they were assumed to have sufficient English to cope with the mainstream program. It is now known that much more fully developed skills in oral and written English are required by these students if they are to be successful in dealing with the academic demands of the program. For them to match the proficiency of their native-English-speaking peers takes more than five years (Cummins 1981, 1984; Wong Fillmore 1983). This should not, however, be interpreted such that students should be kept out of regular classrooms until they have acquired such levels of proficiency. On the contrary, even at the high school level where it is arguably more difficult than in earlier grades for students to cope with the demands of a course designed for proficient users of English, a five-year delay before these students join regular classes would be unthinkable. What is important, however, is that regardless of the instructional setting in which the students are placed, their English-language development is monitored and continuing support offered, if required, for a period of at least five years.

### Students Who Are Valued by the Wider Society Tend to Achieve Better

There is some disturbing evidence from within North America and beyond that societies establish a pecking order in which they rank incoming groups (Skutnabb-Kangas and Toukomaa 1976; Ogbu and Matute-Bianchi 1986). This ranking can be the basis of some powerful self-fulfilling prophecies. School systems often reflect wider societal opinion and thus, perhaps unwittingly, contribute to the perpetuation of lower- or higher-than-justified expectations as to how individual students are likely to achieve.

Decisions regarding how programs and services for second-language learners are to be delivered is one area in which positive action against the fulfillment of such unfounded prophecies can be taken. A model of program delivery that largely separates these students from regular classes carries with it the suggestion that they will be acceptable to the mainstream only when they are unnoticeable within it. It also implies that any different cultural practices and values which these students bring to school with them are of little importance to the school or to the larger society. What is needed to ensure the success of these students is a major effort on the part of the school to indicate clearly to *all* students how much they personally, and the cultural and linguistic group(s) of which they are a part, can contribute to the intellectual and social life of the school. Such demonstration, of course, needs to go far beyond the approach to minority groups that focuses on items such as food, festivals, and famous people!

## What Are the Key Components of a Quality Program?

Given the characteristics of the students involved and the factors already outlined—the link between language and cognitive development, the high levels of English proficiency required, and the effect of social acceptance on achievement—what is called for is a five-point program consisting of the following:

- an orientation program
- a monitoring procedure
- a program of parental involvement
- a language program
- an academic upgrading program

Such a comprehensive program, however, cannot exist in a vacuum. It influences the program for the rest of the students in the school. How other students respond to these second-language learners has a major impact on how well the latter acquire their additional language, succeed in school, and develop socially. Let us look more closely at each of the five program components and then see how the rest of the student body might be involved in the various aspects of the program to ensure its effectiveness.

### An Orientation Program

An orientation program can help new students, their parents, and the staff who will be working with the students.

Students need an orientation to the physical plant and an introduction to key staff members. Basic rules of the school need explaining, including what kind of behavior towards other students and staff is considered acceptable and what is not. A peer who speaks the same language is probably the best choice of person for providing this orientation. At the same time, key words and phrases that will allow the newcomer to get to the washroom, to greet people, and to use politeness formulae can be practiced in English.

For parents, the orientation might contain some basic information about the local school and other schools in the district if optional attendance is available, the various programs and services offered by the district, and the role that parents are encouraged to play. If the parents' English is very limited, it is probably wise to postpone this session until a translator is available. The frame of reference that the parents bring to the situation must be kept in mind while providing the information; if this is not known to the person responsible for the orientation, then it would probably be helpful to start by asking the parents to describe the school environments with which they and their children are familiar.

A good orientation program is a two-way street, with staff gaining as much information as they give. Schools experiencing a fairly large intake of students from any one country would probably want to provide a professional development session to give staff an initial acquaintance with the background of the newcomers. Similarly, schools with substantial numbers of second-generation immigrant students from one or more language/cultural groups would benefit from sessions on culturally influenced childrearing practices and other values held by many members of those groups. Staff who have had this initial kind of orientation will know better how to put parents at ease. The questions staff members ask, too, will more likely be ones which convince parents that the professionals to whom they are about to entrust their children are educated, informed individuals.

## A Monitoring Procedure

A monitoring procedure begins with an initial assessment of a newly registered student, conducted in the language the child understands best, to determine levels of language and academic functioning and to record the student's educational history prior to registration in the present school. Placement and programming recommendations are recorded, with later details of academic, linguistic, and social progress added to that record along with any further assessment information. Whenever it seems appropriate, modifications to placement and programming are made, based on the information collected.

The primary purpose of a monitoring procedure is to help the individual school track student development, paying particular attention to students characterized as being "at risk." A secondary use of this information, collected over a period of time and categorized to allow for comparison across a range of variables, enables the school or district as a whole to gather data useful in describing alternative approaches and assessing their relative effectiveness in educating these students.

## A Program of Parental Involvement

The orientation program referred to earlier is just the beginning of parental involvement. Many immigrant parents who are unfamiliar with North American schooling and whose English is still weak tend to remain on the periphery of their children's education; they rarely respond to school invitations or initiate contact with the school. Children quickly realize that their parents do not know what is happening at school and may take advantage of that fact. Sometimes, too, students lose respect for their parents because they seem incapable of playing the role that English-speaking parents play with the school. On the other hand, research indicates that these same immigrant parents can be an immensely positive factor in their children's success in school if they come to see themselves, and are seen by staff, as co-educators of their children along with the school (Tizard et al. 1982).

An ongoing program of parental involvement begins with finding one area in which the parents will assume some responsibility—for example, reading a bedtime story in whatever language is usually used at home, or helping with a family tree project—and then doing everything possible to ensure that that first contribution is a very satisfying one for both children and parents. Then, staff need to continue tailoring requests for assistance to what seems realistic given the parents' schedules and personalities. Success will be indicated the day the parents suggest a project or activity and ask for *staff* support.

## A Language Program

The aim of a language program should be to *add* English, both oral and written, to the language which the students bring to school, not to *substitute* English for it. It is very easy to give the substitutive message, always referring, for example, to pupils as ESL students instead of as Farsi or Russian speakers or as students who are becoming bilingual. Even worse is to refer to new arrivals or kindergartners as children with *no* language, where clearly, "language" is synonymous with English. An additive program will provide many opportunities for students to display what they can do in their stronger language, and to help others learn at least a little about that language. These students' first languages must be validated within the school setting as powerful tools for thinking, learning, and expressing; if they are not, then we run the risk of not being able to take advantage of what children have learned and can continue to learn through them.

A student's first language is the base on which the second language is built (Swain 1983). Programs for second-language learners that provide a link between their first and subsequent languages have been demonstrated to be very effective both in helping the child acquire the target language and—more importantly—succeed academically (ASCD Panel on Bilingual Education 1987). Teachers, tutors, or peers who are able to speak both languages can increase the pace at and depth to which a new language is acquired, particularly if careful attention is paid to *how* each language is used at different stages in the second-language learning process (Guthrie 1984; Wong Fillmore 1986). Whenever possible, therefore, opportunities for bilingual language programs should be provided.

A good language program also needs to be firmly linked to the academic and social program of the school, with the content of the language program being derived from the language demands made by the regular curriculum, the playground or sports field, and the many other occasions when students/students or students/staff interact during a school day.

Many Creole speakers have been brought up in environments where they have had opportunities to hear English used, particularly in school, at church, and in the broadcast media. Though their productive command of English may be weak, their ability to understand English is superior to that of students who have had no exposure to the language at all. On the other hand, surface similarities between Creole and English may cause these students considerable confusion. Programs designed for Creole speakers have to take these differences into account.

*An Academic Upgrading Program*

Given the lack of opportunities for regular, quality education experienced by many incoming students, a planned program to fill in any gaps in their previous schooling is essential. Academic upgrading, including a basic literacy program, is required for some second-language learners from elementary grades through high school. An academic upgrading program is particularly necessary for supporting efforts to keep students of similar age together in viable instructional groups. Recently arrived immigrant or refugee students who are twelve years old, for example, but who have never been to school or who attended irregularly for a couple of years in overcrowded classrooms with poorly trained teachers, are not going to thrive in a regular Grade 7 classroom without substantial modification to the normal program. In the case of older second-language learners for whom time in school is limited or for others who have a long way to go to catch up with their peers, a bilingual approach to academic upgrading will be most efficient. A bilingual approach allows a teacher or tutor to go over work in the student's dominant language and then to introduce in English some of the key vocabulary and structures required in that work. As the student's proficiency in English improves, the teacher or tutor can begin to use more English, still relying, however, on the student's native tongue to provide a quick check on comprehension whenever necessary. A bilingual approach also makes it more likely that students make explicit links between what they have learned before and what they are learning now. In high schools, bilingual senior students can also contribute to a successful tutoring program, given their recent experience with the material being covered in the courses and their language skills.

Monolingual academic upgrading in English can also be effective, provided the content is carefully matched to the student's academic background and a highly visual and activity-oriented approach is used to ensure comprehension of the material being presented.

In order to ensure both coordination and quality, it is essential that the student's regular teacher be enabled to develop an individual plan for each student. He or she should oversee the implementation of any academic upgrading program in those instances where other instructional staff are involved in its delivery (Johnson 1987).

## Why Is an Integrated Setting Preferable?

A quality program for second-language learners will neither segregate all students until they are "fit" to join their peers, nor will it place them in a regular classroom with the expectation that they will learn all they need to learn on their own. Segregation denies them access to fluent English-speaking models other than their teacher and, therefore, fails to capitalize on an important source of help available in all schools. A mainstreamed placement, without additional support for the students and their teachers, may be successful in the case of already academically proficient and highly motivated students; the rest, however, will flounder. The middle ground, a withdrawal or pull-out program that offers support in a segregated setting for part of the day and mainstreaming for the rest, may seem an ideal compromise. What tends to happen, however, is that everyone, including the student, assumes that the short period of pull-out assistance *is* the learning for the day, and the rest is a kind of marking time until increased proficiency is acquired through the language program.

The ideal is a program that supports second-language students' learning for the entire day. Their instruction would take place mostly within an integrated setting and would segregate them from their English-speaking peers only for the time that is absolutely essential to meet unique learning needs, such as bilingual upgrading programs and programs providing group identity and support. An "integrated setting" (Hester 1984; Rigg and Enright 1986; Enright and McCloskey 1988) can be defined as a class with a mixture of students, some fluent in English, others learning the language, some recently arrived in the country, others born here to parents also born here; it is a classroom that attempts to meet the needs of each group and arranges for opportunities for each to learn something from the other's presence in the class.

In kindergarten–grade 8 settings, what is required is a team of professionals working together to provide the five basic program components listed in this chapter. In such a partnership, second-language teachers would provide their expertise to classroom teachers as to how to teach a second language, classroom teachers would offer their detailed knowledge about the concepts and content to be covered, and other bilingual/bicultural staff and parents would contribute their skills and insights into who these children are, what they know and can do already, and what they need to learn next.

At the high school level, with the added demands of diploma requirements and the increasingly high levels of English proficiency required to cope successfully in regular courses, some greater degree of initial separation of second-language learners into specific instructional groups is, perhaps, inevitable. At the same time, given the need to provide, across a wide range of curriculum areas, content-based credit courses that are tailored to the linguistic and academic needs of second-language learners, there is ample opportunity for collaboration between subject-area specialists and language specialists to design, and perhaps even team-teach, such special subject sections.

This definition of integration suggests that those students learning English are not the only ones to gain from the placement of second-language learners in mainstream classes. For fluent English-speakers, there is the chance to consolidate their academic, social, and language skills by taking the role of tutor from time to time.

Even more impressive are gains that have been documented for all students in the areas of academic achievement, language development, and interethnic, interracial understanding within classrooms that are organized as cooperative learning centers (Goodlad 1984; Kagan 1986). In these classrooms, students from different backgrounds, with differing levels of proficiency in the language of that classroom, and differing levels of academic achievement, are grouped to work together as cooperating teams.

Working side by side also provides for all students unlimited opportunities for cultural enrichment. Teachers who are interested in exploring topics across the curriculum from many different cultural perspectives will welcome the presence of students from a variety of language and cultural backgrounds, and at different stages of adjustment to their new environment. Teachers' recognition of diversity as a rich resource and their acknowledgment of that fact in the public forum of an integrated class is just as important for all other students to hear as it is for those who are being asked to contribute to the learning of the class at any one time.

## Conclusion

Given the large numbers of English-as-a-second-language learners in North American classrooms now and for the foreseeable future, given the length of time it takes for students to become fully proficient in their new language, given the need for continuous monitoring and support during this period of five-plus years, and given the benefits for all students of an integrated instructional setting, there is really only one conclusion that can be reached: every teacher is an English-as-a-second-language teacher, whether assigned to that function or not.

## Acknowledgments

This article began as a briefing paper for the director of the North York Board of Education in May 1986. Evolving versions were presented at conferences in Australia, the United States, Hong Kong, and Canada during 1987–88. With excellent input from members of the North York Board of Education ESL/D Committee and especially its chair, Dr. Marjorie Perkins, it next appeared as a report to the trustees of the North York school board in April 1988. This version has been revised in light of the wider readership for whom it is intended.

## References

Ashworth, M. 1988. *Blessed with Bilingual Brains.* Vancouver: Pacific Educational Press, The University of British Columbia.

Association for Supervision and Curriculum Development Panel on Bilingual Education. 1987. *Building an Indivisible Nation: Bilingual Education in Context.* Alexandria, Va.: Association for Supervision and Curriculum Development.

Brumfit, C., R. Ellis, and J. Levine, eds. 1985. *English as a Second Language in the United Kingdom: ELT Documents 121.* Headington Hill Hall, Oxford: Pergamon Press and The British Council.

Carrington, L. D. 1983. The Challenge of Caribbean Language in the Canadian Classroom. *TESL Talk* 14 (4); 15–28.

Cummins, J. 1981. *Bilingualism and Minority Language Children.* Toronto: The Ontario Institute for Studies in Education.

————. 1984. *Bilingualism and Special Education: Issues in Assessment and Pedagogy.* Clevedon, England: Multilingual Matters.

Donaldson, M. 1978. *Children's Minds.* Glasgow: Collins.

Enright, D. S., and M. L. McCloskey. 1988. *Integrating English: Developing English Language and Literacy in the Multilingual Classroom.* Reading, Mass.: Addison-Wesley.

Goodlad, J. I. 1984. *A Place Called School.* New York: McGraw-Hill.

Guthrie, L. F. 1984. Contrasts in Teachers' Language Use in a Chinese-English Bilingual Classroom. In *On TESOL '83: The Question of Control,* edited by J. Handscombe, R. A. Orem, and B. P. Taylor, 39–52. Washington, D.C.: TESOL.

Hester, H. 1984. Peer Interaction in Learning English as a Second Language. *Theory into Practice* 23 (3): 208–17.

Johnson, D. M. 1987. The Organization of Instruction in Migrant Education: Assistance for Children and Youth at Risk. *TESOL Quarterly* 21 (3): 437–59.

Kagan, S. 1986. Cooperative Learning and Sociocultural Factors in Schooling. In *Beyond Language: Social and Cultural Factors in Schooling Language Minority Students,* California State Department of Education, 231–98. Los Angeles: California State University, Evaluation, Dissemination, and Assessment Center.

Lindfors, J. W. 1987. *Children's Language and Learning.* 2d ed. Englewood Cliffs, N.J.: Prentice-Hall.

McGroarty, M. 1986. Educator's Response to Sociocultural Diversity: Implications for Practice. In *Beyond Language: Social and Cultural Factors in Schooling Language Minority Students,* California State Department of

Education, 299–343. Los Angeles: California State University, Evaluation, Dissemination, and Assessment Center.

Ogbu, J. U., and M. E. Matute-Bianchi. 1986. Understanding Sociocultural Factors: Knowledge, Identity and School Adjustment. In *Beyond Language: Social and Cultural Factors in Schooling Language Minority Students*, California State Department of Education, 73–142. Los Angeles: California State University, Evaluation, Dissemination, and Assessment Center.

Ovando, C., and V. Collier. 1985. *Bilingual and ESL Classrooms*. New York: McGraw-Hill.

Oxford, R., L. Pol, D. Lopez, P. Stupp, S. Peng, and M. Gendell. 1981. *Projections of Non-English Language Background and Limited English Proficient Persons in the United States to the Year 2000*. Rosslyn, Va.: InterAmerica Research Associates.

Rigg, P., and D. S. Enright, eds. 1986. *Children and ESL: Integrating Perspectives*. Washington, D.C.: TESOL.

Skutnabb-Kangas, T., and P. Toukomaa. 1976. *Teaching Migrant Children's Mother Tongue and Learning the Language of the Host Country in the Context of the Sociocultural Situation of the Migrant Family*. Helsinki: The Finnish National Commission for UNESCO.

Swain, M. 1983. Bilingualism without Tears. In *On TESOL '82: Pacific Perspectives on Language Learning and Teaching*, edited by M. A. Clarke and J. Handscombe, 35–46. Washington, D.C.: TESOL.

Tizard, J., W. N. Scholfield, and J. Hewison. 1982. Collaboration between Teachers and Parents in Assisting Children's Reading. *British Journal of Educational Psychology* 52:1–15.

Wells, C. G., and J. Wells. 1984. Learning to Talk and Talking to Learn. *Theory into Practice* 23 (3): 190–97.

Wong Fillmore, L. 1983. The Language Learner as an Individual: Implications of Research on Individual Differences for the ESL Teacher. In *On TESOL '82: Pacific Perspectives on Language Learning and Teaching*, edited by M. A. Clarke and J. Handscombe, 157–73. Washington, D.C.: TESOL.

———. 1986. Research Currents: Equity or Excellence? *Language Arts* 63 (5): 474–81.

# 2  I Grow for a Living

Carole Urzúa
University of the Pacific, Stockton, California

A theology student in preparation for the ministry traveled to neighborhood congregations to work with local pastors. On one such trip he observed the pastor of the local congregation give a children's sermon as part of the regular worship service. All of the children were called to the front of the church and the pastor began his sermon:

"Children, I'm thinking of something that is about five or six inches high; that scampers across the ground; that can climb trees; that lives in either a nest in the tree or makes its home in a hollowed-out portion of a tree's trunk. The thing I'm thinking about gathers nuts and stores them in winter; it is sometimes brown and sometimes gray; it has a big bushy tail. Who can tell me what I'm thinking of?"

Knowing the proper church behavior, the children remained quiet and reserved. No one ventured an answer. Finally, Robert, age 6, slowly and ever so tentatively raised his hand. The pastor, desperate for a response so he could go on with the sermon, said with some relief, "Yes, Robert, what do you think it was?"

"Well," came the response, "ordinarily I'd think it was a squirrel, but I suppose you want me to say it was Jesus" (Harste, Woodward, and Burke 1984).

Context. Perception. It's all in how you look at things. If you're in church, the answer is likely to be Jesus; if you're in school, the answer is squirrel. The same event, the same picture, the same words can all be interpreted in different ways, depending on a complex set of variables such as background, intelligence, relationship, time of day, location, or previous encounters. Remember Psychology 101 in which the professor asked you to look at a picture, and one moment you saw an old woman with a long nose, and the next moment you saw a young woman with a feather in her long hair? Which did you see first? What did you have to do to see the other image? Psychologists tell us it is more than just "looking"; your mind has to accommodate to the second image before you can actually see it.

15

## Multiple Perceptions of Second-language Children

In the last few years, it has become clear to me that children in schools, particularly minority children in schools, may be victims of this multiple perception situation. One perception begins at home. By the family, a language-minority child is generally viewed as someone to be socialized, loved, respected, and accepted. At age five the child goes to school. Administrators have other perceptions. They might see the child as either a number that will bring more federal dollars to the program, as a welcome addition to a rich multicultural environment, or, perhaps, as an entity to be fudged on so the numbers don't add up to the required level for a bilingual program. The child is assigned to a classroom. In fact, many of our children are assigned to many classrooms, frequently as a result of their poverty, or their inability to speak English, or their being members of families which are in the migrant stream. Many of our children are, therefore, assigned to a mainstream classroom teacher, a Chapter 1 teacher, an ESL teacher, a migrant teacher, perhaps even a special education teacher. Each of these teachers may see the child in a different way. Because of the training, the motivation for teaching, and the particular group of colleagues they work with, among other things, each teacher brings a unique set of expectations and attitudes to the perception of minority children.

I was moved by an article in a newsmagazine, which suggested that there are new insights in various scientific communities by virtue of the fact that women are entering the fields and asking new questions. In the field of primatology, for example, a field dominated by men who have studied how dominant primates fight, mate, and decide who would reproduce, women are changing the picture. When women primatologists study, for example, langurs, they emphasize behaviors other than those involving the male—for example, female hierarchies and mother-child interaction—and thus draw a richer picture of a primate society (*Newsweek* Dec. 2, 1985, p. 84).

What affected me in this article was the realization that the very questions one chooses to research determine what kind of perspective others will have of the reality being observed. Thomas Kuhn (1962) said it more eloquently: "The prevailing paradigm in a science depends not only on experimental truths, but also on the scientific communities' shared beliefs" (1962). And so in this chapter I'd like to pose this question for us: Are the shared beliefs of all the communities responsible for the education of minority children the same? Does the mainstream teacher, socialized and educated in elementary education programs or content-specific certification programs, approach the teaching of minority children in the same way that the second-language teacher, socialized and educated in ESL or bilingual programs, does?

I think not.

The differences in the teaching approaches have come from the fact that the community which educates teachers for first-language instruction has been asking questions and researching answers that, in general, the community which educates teachers for second-language instruction has not been aware of. And the reverse is also true. Because the questions have frequently been different and have rarely been shared with the opposite community, two different paradigms have resulted. I am stunned by how little my colleagues in TESOL and bilingual education know about the active, exciting research and application in the area of first-language arts. And I am equally stunned by the ignorance my colleagues in elementary, language arts, and reading education have concerning the fascinating observations being made in second-language classrooms. If, therefore, we are to truly make education for minority children not just equal, but possessing quality, we all—first-language, mainstream, as well as second-language teachers—must know what the other communities are doing and what kinds of questions they are asking.

In the rest of this chapter, therefore, I'd like to share some important findings in the language teaching field, findings from both first- and second-language educators. To those readers who are essentially mainstream teachers who have minority children in classrooms, I'd like to share several research findings and concomitant applications in the field of second-language learning. And to those who are second-language teachers in bilingual settings, or who are ESL or Chapter 1 teachers with specific responsibilities for non-native-English-speaking children, I'd like to share some important insights from research with native-English-speaking children. Ultimately, I hope we can all look at our children, and know that by broadening our knowledge as their teachers, we can see them as what they are—children. Not disadvantaged children. Not LEP children. Not even brown or black or yellow children. But as children. They deserve our best efforts to ask all the possible questions regarding their education so that, as their advocates, we can formulate a shared set of beliefs.

## Insights from Second-language Study

*Language Is Learned through Communication*

The first aspect which the community of second-language teachers and researchers can teach us has to do with a basic tenet of language learning: people learn language because they are in real situations where communicating is valued. As Enright and McCloskey have said (1985), and I have written about also (1981), when activities are designed that allow children to persuade and inform, question and argue about their own intentions, they have purpose for their acquisition.

To give you a concrete, classroom example of the expectation of purposefulness, come with me to a sixth grade classroom of twenty-two Hmong, five black, two Hispanic, and a couple of white children where a student teacher is holding forth from the grammar book. Having spent half the period with a fast-paced lecture on prepositional phrases of place, she proceeds to assign a writing activity: write a paragraph describing your room at home, saying where everything is placed in the room, thus resulting, in her mind, in such prepositional phrases as "on the wall" and "beside the bed." The children take the assignment seriously, but when the student teacher asks, "Why are you going to write this paragraph?" she is surprised by the answer: "Are you coming to visit us?" Her response is to remind students that they are practicing prepositional phrases.

My response was to gasp at the nature of this child's understanding: "If we're being asked to write something, it must be important, and someone will want to know if what we're writing is true." The children's belief in the value of communicating with a real audience about an experience which has intrinsic value changed the student teacher's view of the assignment. Thus, the next day, the children read their paragraphs to two or three friends who, first independently and then collectively, drew diagrams of the room being described by the author. The natural feedback, and the ensuing discussion, created a purpose for revision. It was almost as good as visiting in their homes!

Another aspect of this need for authentic, communicative activities is that children need to be in situations where, in order to be successful, communication must take place. Sometimes we generate good activities in which children work side by side with no interaction, or more assertive children dominate the experience. Thus, if all of us are to help forge a new paradigm of language and learning, we must create situations in which success is dependent upon talking.

A good example of this kind of activity is a box with a hand-sized hole on either end into which interesting objects are placed. The task is for two learners to each insert a hand and talk to each other about the contents. Successful experiences, thus, are based on mutually communicating about the problem; the tasks simply cannot be done with only one person talking! (See Urzúa 1981 for further ideas.)

Finally, the need for authentic, valuable activities relates to the need for cognitive content, not linguistic syllabi. Although second-language teachers of old did use linguistic form to drive their scope and sequences, there has been a movement toward using content material as the outline for classes, particularly because research shows that children require five to seven years to learn a language (Cummins 1981), and they, therefore, should be surrounded by interesting, supportive materials and instruction during this time.

Curriculum writers are beginning to address this issue. In a recent text for children, for example, there are several units about dinosaurs (Hudelson 1985). Throughout these units, children will learn about factors contributing to the demise of dinosaurs, as well as comparisons of weight, height, eating habits, and habitats. Since this kind of information is communicated through reading selections (sometimes in somewhat abstract language), the students do many activities before they actually read. Therefore, the text directs students to do the following things, over a period that may extend into a week or two: in groups of two or three, they will put various dinosaur skeletons together when given tagboard cut-outs of bones; they will make clay models of a certain dinosaur, given pictures and the previous skeletons; they will read a short selection about one of the dinosaurs, and then in those same small groups, discuss what information about their dinosaur is salient to teach their classmates, in order to create a class chart comparing various dinosaurs on the criteria suggested above. (This idea is called the "Jigsaw" by Aaronson et al. 1978.) Finally, the students will play a modification of the game Clue in which various dinosaurs die off in various continents because of various factors. All of the aspects of communicative language pedagogy which I have mentioned are thus embodied in these activities: the activities are real and authentic, not contrived for a school setting; the activities require children to talk to one another in order to be successful; and the content of the activities is cognitively defensible, and is drawn from academic disciplines found in schools.

## Attitude Affects Language Learning

A second aspect which the community of second-language teachers and researchers can teach us about has to do with the importance of affect on learning, and particularly on language learning. There is quite a large body of research on how a learner's attitude affects the language learned. Perhaps you can recall a personal experience when you have been actively, passionately involved in an experience from which you learned a great deal; chances are the affect was positive, supportive, encouraging, confident. You were not threatened in any way. Krashen (1982) would say your affective filter, through which all learning permeates, was very low.

Thus research, substantiated by our own experiences in learning second languages, corroborates the fact that learning is an affective experience. When we deal with minority children, then, it's important to remember that success breeds further success. Do successful experiences happen often for our children?

Perhaps not. The dropout rates among language-minority children are far higher than any others. It would seem that the findings of second-language researchers and teachers are not always adhered to.

But it's not exactly clear what the problems are. There are no good and bad sides in this area, particularly when we begin to ask ourselves what kind of role we must play as teachers. How can we balance the knowledge and the belief in a supportive, successful environment with the demands of a school system for competency tests and grade-level equivalencies? I think we have to return to effective second-language pedagogy to find some answers.

## Language Learning Involves Choice

First, effective second-language teachers have taught all of us—first- and second-language educators—that the learner is the one responsible for choosing whom she or he will interact with; when learners make these choices for themselves, they are then open to receiving the comprehensible input they need to learn. Learners decide. Learners choose. Even when you are using your native language, you make these choices all the time. What, then, is the effect of coming to school and being told either that there is only one person from whom you can learn (the teacher), or that if you are allowed to interact at all, the teacher will decide with whom it will be? Second-language teachers sometimes moan that their new immigrant children will not speak to them, even after several months of schooling. The teachers project their own frustration onto the child, and often make assumptions that there is something wrong with the child, or that the teacher is not doing his or her duty. Neither may be the case. Remember, the learner chooses.

One little kindergartner I observed several years ago made an interesting choice. The only person she would have anything to do with for almost six months was the teacher. With extraordinary adroitness, the teacher balanced the needs this child had with those of the other eighteen five-year-olds; of over 600 initiations of this child during a five-hour observation period, the teacher was unresponsive only eight percent of the time. Much of the time, the teacher recognized that since the child was getting her primary input from her, she had a responsibility to maintain the interaction and ultimately engender a positive affect concerning the use of language. Notice, for example, how the teacher in this interaction displays a certain expectation that if the two of them just keep going, they will eventually understand one another.

*Child:* I got a bathing suit . . . a new one.
*Adult:* You have a what?
*Child:* A bathing suit.
*Adult:* Soup?
*Child:* A bathing suit.
*Adult:* Baby soap?
*Child:* Bathing suit.
*Adult:* What do you do with it?
*Child:* I put it on and go swimming. That's what—
*Adult:* A bathing suit! You put it on and you go swimming.
*Child:* Uh huh. It's a new one. I can't wear it.

The teacher thus says, in effect, "If you're going to choose to speak to me, we will make the best of it."

Although she validated the choice her little friend made about interacting only with her, the teacher also recognized that if the child was to have the opportunity to link up with other children, both sides would have to be socialized into appropriate behavior. Therefore, frequently the teacher played the role of a facilitator/translator/interpreter between this little girl and her classmates.

In one interchange, for example, the little girl came to join the circle of children sitting on the rug, but found no place to sit. She stood passively behind the circle, until the teacher said, "S＿＿＿ needs a place to sit down. Where could she sit?" Several holes were made for the child to sit down; the teacher had, in effect, been the voice for the request of this little child.

At other times, the teacher wanted to convey the attitude that it was the other children's responsibility to try to understand what their friend wanted to communicate. In one particularly frustrating interaction which followed the making of bird feeders, the teacher demonstrated to everyone that the girl was doing her best to tell them what she wanted, and it was their collective responsibility to try to understand.

*Teacher:* Did you hang it in a tree?

*Child:* Uh, uh. [No.] Put it in, hm, there. [Gestures like hanging something.]

*Teacher:* Where?

*Child:* I don't know.

*Teacher:* Not in a tree?

*Child:* I don't know. A-a-a

*Teacher:* Hm. By the window?

*Child:* Nope.

*Teacher:* No. By the door?

*Child:* Nope.

*Teacher:* [to the other children] She needs a word to tell me where she put it.

*Boy:* From the roof?

*Teacher:* From the roof, Drew says? From the roof?

*Child:* [Turns to look at Drew]     (Urzúa 1977–78)

In this instance, then, we see a concerned caregiver who allows the learners to choose whom they will talk to, and also one who becomes a facilitator to help the learner make interactive links.

## Putting the Language onto the Concepts

There is a second effective technique used by second-language teachers who practice aspects of affective teaching. The technique involves departing from the stylized, school-culture, question-answer-response interchanges and moving to a more conversational tone, where the teacher's language provides the affective bridge between what the child knows cognitively and what the target language linguistically encodes. The result is a patter of language that reflects what the child, or sometimes the teacher, is doing. It is a technique I have called "milieu teaching." Instead of questioning a child about the color he or she is using to paint a picture, milieu teachers would observe, "Oh, look at how much red you used in your picture. A red tree, a red car, and a red sun. You must like red." Evidence suggests that a perfect language learning situation is created when the teacher's comments are accompanied by affective aspects such as eye contact, a smile, and perhaps a touch. (See Wells 1981.)

In one classroom I worked in, the children were preparing to make mobiles by interviewing one another concerning their favorite things, then drawing and cutting out magazine pictures to demonstrate their preferences, which had been written on a large chart. One girl newly arrived from Vietnam had cut out several pictures and had laid them out on the table in front of her. I sat down beside her, and directed her attention to the chart.

> *Me:*   Chin, let's look up there and see. "Read a book" is your favorite thing, so you have a picture of a book. And you have another picture of a book here [pointing to each picture], and you're happy when you read your book, so you made lots of happy faces, and you do not like to ride a boat and it makes you sick when you ride a boat. You don't have a picture of anybody who's sick. Can you find a picture of somebody who's sick?
>
> *Chin:*   [Points to a picture of bodies lying on the ground]
>
> *Me.*   Oh, that's what that was. People who are sick.

You might argue that there is too much teacher talk! But I would argue that in this concrete situation of cutting and pasting, with a new learner of a second language (L2), the most efficient use of the teacher is to establish a warm bonding experience in which language is used to code the actions, experiences, or even thoughts a child might be having. Thus, in this experience, or milieu, I am reviewing the task and noting the results, rather than quizzing the child and forcing her to speak in situations where she may not choose to do so. If, for example, the child was actually unaware of the English vocabulary for *book* or *boat*, and if I had quizzed the child about these words, I would have only reinforced a belief that teachers know all the words and the main task of the learner is to guess and learn them. Or perhaps even more crucial to the affective role of the interactants, I would have ignored the fact that language learning is essentially a social process.

By contrast, in milieu teaching, I have actually reinforced the underlying assumption that Chin and I are involved in a conversation, even though Chin does not use oral language. I assumed that actions are meaningful and are potentially responsive, such as when Chin points to a picture in response to my request that she find pictures in the magazine which illustrate sick people. Whenever there is any kind of a response by a child, I assume that that is a turn in a conversation, and respond as if the child had indeed given a meaningful conversational utterance. Caregivers in first-language situations do this frequently; as Snow says, by carrying on both sides of a conversation, caregivers teach their infants the rules of interacting (1977).

*Summary*

We can summarize, then, what second-language teachers and researchers are contributing to our understanding of effective language teaching practices: (1) application of the principle that language is learned when authentic communication takes place often results in active, real projects where successful completion of the activity is dependent upon talking; (2) application of the principle that language learning has a major affective component often results in allowing learners to be in control of their learning by choosing with whom they will interact, and also by teachers playing a mediating role for children who may choose not to interact at certain times. It also results in establishing a bond and in assuming that all actions by children are meaningful and can be translated into facilitating words by the teacher.

## Insights from First-language Study

Now, what about the contributions being made by first-language scholars and teachers? What are some of the questions being asked that can contribute to a shared paradigm for effectively teaching minority children? To me, the most important contributions are in the areas of literacy.

*Reading Research*

In the last twenty years, schools have often adopted a perspective on literacy that goes something like this: reading is a set of skills that can be taught and mastered in a predetermined sequence; when these skills are mastered, the accumulation of such components will produce comprehension of the author's message.

This has sometimes been called a bottom-up theory because it emphasizes letters before words, words before sentences, sentences before paragraphs. It is frequently seen in literacy instruction through phonic workbooks and skills such as "getting the main idea."

But anyone who has spent time observing what readers really do when they process print knows that such a view of reading trivializes the power of the human propensity to make sense of spoken and written language. The first kid-watcher to make this claim was Kenneth Goodman (1967), who calls reading a "psycholinguistic guessing game" in which the reader takes into account a number of language systems in order to predict what the author is trying to say. Knowledge of the pragmatic, semantic, syntactic, and phonological systems allows readers to sample the written system for cues to the meaning; when the predictions don't fit the rest of the sentence, readers return and rethink the ways in which they have responded. These returns are prompted by whether the material being read makes sense. An example of how this works can be seen in the reading of a sixth grade boy with whom I interacted in a research study I conducted. (Urzúa 1987; Rigg 1986). The boy was reading a story called "Winter Olympics." After reading the first paragraph about snow and ice, he read:

*Reader:* The winter
*Text:*   To win a gold medal. . . .

Using what he knows about discourse (i.e., if the piece is about winter, predicting that the word *winter* will be used), what he knows about graphophonics (i.e., t–win), what he knows about syntax (i.e., the most common sentence pattern begins with a noun phrase, frequently the subject, *the winter*), this child has sampled and predicted on very logical, well-informed grounds. But in this case, the reading matter does not match his prediction; Goodman would say he has been miscued by the information he has matched with the text. Because his miscue results in a structure that does not make sense, he returns and reads the sentence again, this time reading what is printed in the text.

As we see in this example, the miscues of readers are seldom random. The active use of cueing systems, and the propensity for creating sense, sometimes misleads us, but none of us read haphazardly, and we all need to be allowed to guess, hypothesize, and try things out in order to construct the meaning. This process, by the way, is not different from the ways in which we learn oral language; we must be active constructors, hypothesizers, risk-takers to put things together in ways that convey our intended meanings.

This psycholinguistic view of the reading process reveals a powerful human ability. There are some researchers/teachers who have applied miscue analysis to children reading in their second language (see Rigg 1986; Hudelson 1981), but, unfortunately, only a few second-language teachers are familiar with the vast research done in this field. Armed with outdated information and models of education that sometimes see minority children as deficient in their abilities simply because they do not speak English, second-language educators in the past have created programs that are even more oriented towards skills and control than those written for first-language children. For example, Bereiter and Englemann (1966), making the assumptions that minority children have no language, and what they have is illogical, created one of the most bizarre programs ever for teaching minority children to read: DISTAR. Because it is labeled as a program that will help minority, "disadvantaged" children, many of us—first- and second-language teachers—have bought the idea that particularly "these" children must have careful, linear lessons of phonic rules and skill tasks.

What informed, meaning-centered first-language teachers would have us know, however, is that DISTAR and other programs like it are the exact opposite of what we must offer our ESL children. If children are to trust their growing knowledge of the meaning-construction process, and if they are to learn how to use the specific cueing systems of their second language, then they must have even more opportunities than first-language children to read authentic texts with meaningful content that matches, as closely as possible, their own background knowledge. Let me demonstrate how that can happen.

As part of my research study with four Southeast Asian children, I asked them to read from a series of reading selections. The results have been analyzed in depth by Rigg (1986); it is her analysis I would like to share.

Figure 1 illustrates the reading of the sixth grade boy named Khamla, the same reader who predicted *the winter*. Khamla is Laotian and is not literate in his native language.

The markings are those of an analysis called the "reading miscue inventory" (Goodman and Burke 1972). Without going into the mechanics of the inventory itself, I'd like to share a few of Rigg's insights. First of all, Khamla read this piece with considerable sound-letter accuracy, as in his substitutions of *natives* for *nations*, *$granther* for *gather*, *greater* for *gather*, *$hatalet* for *athlete*. (The $ denotes a non-English word.) In fact, when completely measured, Khamla's graphic similarity score is 83 on a scale of 0–100, rather high, according to Rigg. The resulting sentences, however, make little sense and don't sound like English. For example, "Every four years young men and women of the world natives $granther at the Winter $Ollgon."

Every four years young men and women of

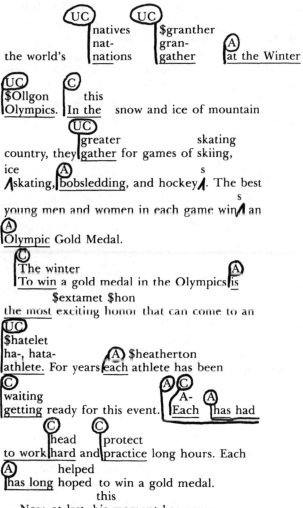

the world's ...

A—Reader repeated that section of the text. C—Reader regressed and successfully attempted to match the text. UC—Reader regressed and unsuccessfully attempted to match the text. $—A non-English word. ⋏—Addition by reader.

Figure 1. Khamla's Reading Miscue Inventory (Rigg 1986)

As part of the reading miscue inventory, students are asked to retell the whole story; the retelling gives a rough suggestion of comprehension at a global level. Khamla's retelling score is 33, again on a 0–100 scale, and when the miscues are figured per hundred words, his score is 25. That is, he miscued an average of every fourth word, a significant problem. Some of us may have ended our analysis here, assumed that Khamla was not able to read at this level of text because we had observed his slow, painful reading, and assigned him to more skills work, perhaps on comprehension "skills" like getting the main idea. But Rigg points out two further pieces of information that we must not overlook. First of all, Khamla struggles to correct many of his miscues in an attempt to build meaning. He is successful twenty percent of the time, as in:

| | |
|---|---|
| *Khamla:* | In this snow and ice . . . |
| *Text:* | In the snow and ice . . . |
| *Khamla:* | The winter |
| *Text:* | To win a gold medal. |

He tries on twenty percent of the other miscues and is unsuccessful, as we see in the first sentence of Figure 1.

But even more important is the evidence Rigg finds of Khamla's abilities in a second piece he had read at the same time as he read "Winter Olympics." In this piece, Khamla's miscues per hundred words were only 12.5, and his graphic similarity 70. And when he retold this story, he scored a perfect 100, an unusual experience, according to Rigg. What made the difference?

The other reading Khamla did was a piece called "The Wise Father." The central character is a father mouse who wants to find a husband for his daughter; after interviewing the sun, a cloud, the wind, and a wall, he decides that the most suitable suitor is a mouse, since it is more powerful than all these, being able to nibble through a wall. The structure of this story is one we all recognize: the central character has a goal and overcomes repeated obstacles in order to reach that goal. The obstacles that the father overcomes are very similar: each time he thinks he has found the perfect mate for his daughter, he is told, "There is something more powerful than I." Thus, not only are the events repetitious, but so are the phrases. The story structure itself, then, helps to teach the reader; the reader is alerted by the sentence, "There is something more powerful than I," that the mouse is going to repeat that same event. Thus, the reader grows in the ability to predict what is going to come next. After reading the encounter that the mouse has with the sun, it is easier to read the encounter he has with a cloud, and that makes it easier still to read the encounter with the wind, and so on. The predictability of event and language, then, makes the construction of meaning a much easier process. The more predictable the text, the more likely it is that the reader will construct the meaning, and not be so fixated on the graphophonic system.

"Winter Olympics," by contrast, is a poorly written piece, taken from a basal reader (the graded series of readers used in elementary schools in the United States). As we see in the transcript of the text, the piece begins like those found in elementary school social studies texts. The reader grows to expect more information about the Olympics, since the story uses habitual action in the present tense. But in the second sentence of the second paragraph, the tense, and thus the meaning, shifts: "For years, each athlete has been getting ready for his event." And even more jarring is one sentence in the third paragraph: "Now, at last, his moment has come." Who is *he*? How did we get from an expository piece on the Olympics to an on-the-spot description of the inner feelings of one "he"? That Khamla was able to get even a score of 33 on the retelling seems to be somewhat of a miracle!

It is difficult to escape the conclusion that reading ability is not just a case of you have it or you don't. All of us, first- and second-language readers alike, bring to a literacy task the expectation to construct meaning. We use everything we know about language, about structures, about oral traditions, and about our cultures. When the reading texts, and the reading tasks, are somewhat congruent with what we know, we are able to use our powerful processes to their maximum. When the texts and the tasks divert us from our purpose, either by being random, with chaotic language and structure, or by forcing us to fixate on one of the cueing systems to the exclusion of the others, then we, like Khamla in his reading of "Winter Olympics," become disabled readers.

What, then, can we learn from meaning-centered first-language teachers that will help our children? First of all, our children should read silently from self-chosen books *every day*. In fact, a wonderful idea used by many schools is "sustained silent reading," in which everyone, from the janitor to the principal to the teacher, takes time off at a prearranged time each day to read. When children see adults reading their own selected texts for enjoyment, children see modeled the very behavior that will be advantageous to them.

Second, there should be some payoff for reading and constructing meaning, such as sharing a favorite part of a story with your friend. Or reading something on Tyrannosaurus Rex to talk about in class because the class is going to build a chart on dinosaurs. Answering questions the teacher poses is not a payoff; creating your own questions is.

Third, the reading materials that our children read, especially at first, need to be the most predictable we can find, such as children's fairytales, pattern stories, and songs. Many of the fine predictable stories, available through Scholastic and The Wright Group in the Big Books, can be read by a whole group of kids at the same time. Many teachers I visited in Australia made their own Big Books from their favorite children's books, and then laminated them.

And finally, much of what children read should be their own words, especially through language experience. There can be nothing more predictable than to read what you have just written, or what a scribe has written for you. Meaning-centered language teachers find innovative ways of making sure every child gets many opportunities to read by inviting senior citizens into the classroom, arranging with teachers of other grade levels to have some of the children visit for a while, and even getting hooked up with students at local community colleges and universities who may be doing practicum experiences. In addition to being scribes and listeners, of course, these volunteers in the classroom can read to children from these same wonderful pieces of literature you've accumulated for the children to read. No one outgrows the need for, and interest in, being read to.

*Writing*

This last method, that of using children's own language for the language experience stories, brings us to another major influence in first-language teaching/learning that is just beginning to make its way into second-language settings. This is the interest in the writing process. Research of the past decade has really transformed the kinds of questions being asked concerning this composing process. Begun by scholars observing both their own and their adult students' processes, it has become fascinatingly clear that through written language we come to know what is potentially knowable to ourselves; the composing process, then, is another way of constructing meaning. As one of my favorite authors, May Sarton says, "I have written every poem, every novel, for the same purpose—to find out what I think, to know where I stand" (1973, 12).

The process is a messy one; it begins with frantic first-draft writing, moves back and forth to reorganizing, rewriting, and rethinking, and ends with a dispassionate careful editing into more standard format.

It is not linear. It is often painful and frustrating. It is a layering of words that say what is desired, with words that say what is desired to a particular audience and with a particular style. It is hard work.

On the positive side are the results of daily writing that young children experience. Work by Graves (1983) with English-as-a-first-language children, and Edelsky (1986), Hudelson (1986), and my own work (1987) with English-as-a-second-language children have shown conclusively that (1) children can begin writing long before they are in formal reading classes, and in fact, children can learn to read by writing; (2) children learn to write in a variety of modes and for a variety of purposes by being free to write whatever they wish. In fact, children from the ages of two and three put pen to paper in meaningful ways, and by the time they come to kindergarten are very aware of the wealth of language seen in environmental print such as that on boxes, signs, labels, and directions; (3) children are significantly influenced by the attitudes of their teachers towards composing. If teachers understand writing as work in progress, not as products that always use correct spelling and grammar, the students' work will reflect those assumptions.

Interestingly, with only individual attention to such things as spelling and sentence construction that occur in unique form in each paper, children, in fact, learn the mechanics of writing as well or better than those who have concentrated on mastery of skill tasks (Kreeft et al. 1984). In one school district I observed, the first graders who participated in writing every day and who used language experience and predictable books actually did better on many sections of the achievement tests than other first graders who had spent their whole year in phonics books and basal readers. The additional benefit for these meaning-centered children, of course, is that they, in addition, read well, write for purposes, interact through the printed word with many different people, and enjoy literacy. Most importantly, it takes very little on the part of the reader/responders to influence writers to change, revise, and rethink their written pieces until they truly say what they want to say.

The influence of reader response on a writer's revision was especially obvious in an observational study I conducted in the school year 1983–84. My colleague, ESL teacher Sue Braithwaite, and I met with four children weekly for forty-five minutes. We had two sixth grade boys, one Cambodian and one Laotian, and two fourth grade girls, both Cambodian. Because we believed in the composing process research in first-language settings, we believed the same results could be replicated in second-language children. The children wrote at home and brought their pieces to writing groups where they read aloud what they had written and we responded to their piece. We emphasized the necessary aspect of the revision process and the goal of communicating their meaning. Careful analysis of the products and the process surprised even me.

Because of the immediacy of the audience feedback, the peer response group appears to have had a dramatic influence on writing development. One of several things the children developed was a sense of audience. Largely through questions they asked the writers, the children came to trust their friends' interest in the topic, and in their own sense of finding their own voice.

One of the best examples of this process was a revision made by one of the boys, Vuong. The task for this piece was to write about a self-chosen topic. Both of the boys chose to write personal narratives about their experiences at Outdoor School, a sixth grade camping experience with their classmates to observe and conduct science and ecology experiments, as well as participate in the traditional camping experiences of roasting marshmallows and going for hikes. (Vuong's first draft can be seen on the left-hand side in Figure 2.) While Vuong read his paper to us twice, we all took notes about anything we wanted to remember to tell him. Then we each took turns reading from our notes. As you can see in Figure 3, much of the input from the other children was in the form of questions about things they wanted to have more information about. Vuong's oral responses are in the second column, and the notes he took for himself during or after we spoke to him are in column three.

What was the impact of this audience input on the second draft, which Vuong did at home? The second draft showed how significant the feedback from Vuong's audience was to the revision process. He added more information, clarified, and expanded on information he already had, all at the appropriate place, and all without any indication from teachers or friends as to where these revisions should occur. The first question, for example, "How was it on the boat when you crossed the river?" stimulated Vuong to orally respond: "It was scared. You know, foggy, deep water. The water is green." Jotting down into his notes only the words, *Information cross the river*, Vuong, nevertheless, makes a significant revision in his second draft, one that adds similar information to that which he had answered orally over a week before.

Although the second draft is clearly not yet an interesting, cohesive account of his experience, we were the most excited about this one revision because it represented an enormous breakthrough for Vuong.

**First Draft**

First we got to the river we have to cross the river. On boat and we got to the camp and we pick up our stuff after that and we have to carry our stuff up to the cabin. Then we take our clothes out of the bags and get ready for dinner. After that it was campfire. Everyday we went hiking and we have to take notes. I went cascade hike we saw a woodpecker it was fun hike finally we on top of the mountain it was so scared. We saw some plants on the road it was tired hike finally we get to eat lunchs. I made my self four sandwiches boy it was good. It was a beautiful day we can see everywhere.

**Second Draft**

When we arrive to outdoor school and all of us cross the river. The water was deep it was green water it has plants in it. When we arrive to other side we have to wait for peoples to cross the river. And then we walk to cafeteria and get our bags and we to the cabin and take our clothes out of the bag and put it on my feet. And we went down to eat lunchs after lunchs we have to sing a song so we can dismiss.

Then we went to hiking it was a long hike we were so tired finally it was lanchs time on the top of the mountain. And we come back form the mountain. It was dinner time after that it was campfire each cabin have to make up a skit to show each other. When I get there I felt happy when you have to live I felt say. On the last day we had breakfast in bed we had coffee cakes eggs and oranges.

Figure 2. Vuong's First and Second Drafts (Urzúa 1987)

Few, if any, changes had ever been made on subsequent drafts of any of his previous pieces. His idea of revision had been to copy, one word at a time, onto a clean sheet of paper, being careful to avoid cross-throughs or sloppy penmanship. On one such revision, for example, the words were even placed on the page in a similar fashion. His revision of the outdoor experience, therefore, represents his first real understanding of the purpose for writing: to communicate something of importance to an audience.

One of the gratifying results of this study is that I am finding the same observations made by Graves (1983) and Calkins (1983) about English-as-a-first-language children to be true about students who had been learning English as a second language for only a short time and who were not literate in their native tongue. Kreeft and colleagues (1984) found similar results in an NIE study of second-language children exchanging written comments with the teacher in what are called dialogue journals. In dialogue journals, students initiate and expand on any topic of interest to them; the teacher responds,

| Peer Response | Writer's Response | Writer's Notes |
|---|---|---|
| 1. How was it on the boat when you crossed the river? | It was scared. You know, foggy, deep water. The water is green. | Information cross the river. |
| 2. Was it a little boat or a big boat? Did it take some people and then come back and get other people? | Oh. Ten people at a time. | 10 people at a time |
| 3. Where do you put the clothes? "What clothes?" The clothes that you wear. | Oh, under our bed. No, in the bag. In your bag, you know, you can put below your foot, feet. Put below your feet when you are sleeping. | |
| 4. He didn't tell us what you do in camp-fire. | | More on campfire. |
| 5. The first part seemed to be the first impression that you had of the camp. But I didn't know it was camp. So what you need to say is, "When I arrived at camp . . ." and then go on and say what you did. | | When we arrive |
| 6. [talking about crossing the river] It would have made me a little more involved in your story if you had said how you felt. | | How I felt |

Figure 3. Peer Response Group Session

questions, and initiates as appropriate, resulting in a written conversation. Kreeft suggests that when written interaction occurs, children focus on the message and learn the forms as they occur in the written exchanges.

*Summary*

To summarize the contributions of first-language, meaning-centered educators to our understanding of effective language teaching practices: learning to read and to write seem mainly dependent on whole, authentic texts which are written for real audiences and read for real purposes. When learners feel the written page has sense, as Frank Smith says (1985), literacy takes care of itself.

So it would seem we've covered all of our bases. We know that the combined questions and contributions of both first-language and second-language communities can forge a more complete paradigm of shared beliefs.

But I'm uncomfortable. It would be unfortunate for me to leave the impression that we are exclusively concerned with our children as language learners, because ultimately and primarily, we are concerned with them as learners, learners who through their natural growth and development require certain things in order to be healthy, effective people in their society of schooling. Their main task, then, is not to be learners of languages. What do they think is important?

My poet friend Kim Stafford asked a group of third grade children to put themselves into the place of something or someone else and see what it felt like. One boy imagined himself as a tree and reflected, "I grow for a living."

Growing for a living. That's what our learners' major task is, in and out of school. And what does that growing look like? There is, of course, a great deal known about how human beings learn, and what kind of environment supports that learning. That would seem to be the stuff of another paper! But let me follow just one strand to demonstrate how we might encourage our children to grow for a living.

From Piaget we know that human beings are constantly reworking, reorganizing, rearranging data of all kinds so that the very organizing principles, or schema, in our brains are constantly shifting. To say learning has taken place, then, is to acknowledge that the brain has recognized something in a new way. It is not simply a matter of having taken something in and mapped it onto our old self; the new thinking relates to everything else we have in an individual way. Indeed, each aspect of learning is unique because of the previous schema we possess; those schema predispose us to see the world in a certain way, and they also provide the boundaries, so to speak, of where the learning will fit.

What is an implication of this understanding? All of us who have contact with our second-language learners must encourage them to be active agents in their learning, self-starters in their approach to schooling tasks, questioners in their approach to all they do. We must engage our children, in all aspects of their schooling, with the attitude of "What is it you understand?" *not* "Did you take in what I just told you?" Even something as supposedly linear as mathematics is based on principles that must be learned, not memorized. Asking children, "What is it you understand about this problem?" is to try to see how the learning they have done is progressing. Only if and when we are part of their learning enterprise can we truly say we are contributing to their growth.

Frank Smith was once asked if it was possible to conduct the language classroom he advocates with thirty children. His answer illuminates our understanding of helping children to grow. He said that it may be difficult to do what he, Smith, was advocating. But, ultimately, "the human brain . . . will not alter its nature to suit the contingencies of the classroom. The way children learn is the way children learn, no matter what pressures and constraints are laid upon teachers in classrooms. Schools are a different kind of reality, determined not so much by the nature of children's brains (whatever we might sentimentally like to think) but by the day-to-day exigencies of maintaining the existence and smooth running of bureaucratically organized institutions" (1983, 137).

I would like to think we might prove him wrong. I would like to hope that "bureaucratically organized institutions" might develop a new paradigm for dealing with all children, but particularly with minority children. When we hear some teacher who has been assigned twenty-two Cambodian children begin her sentences with, "These children can't . . ." perhaps we can take some of the emerging data from our researchers and put a published article in that teacher's mailbox. Or when we hear someone talk about the "poor LEPS" (limited English proficient speakers) who have so many problems in school, perhaps we can remind that person that there are very few people in the world who have failed to learn a native language, one of the most complex tasks known to human endeavor, and that all of our ESL children have, in fact, learned a native language. Yet our schools sometimes make our children appear to have a problem because they do not speak English. The problem is the schools', not the children's. Or when we hear administrators talk about busing our children to centers to learn English before they can become mainstreamed, perhaps we can remind them that if the children are to become good users of English, and good citizens to boot, they must have a reason to learn the language. Hooking them up with buddies in mainstream classes who are more proficient than they are is a guaranteed acquisition environment; someone needs to be more linguistically proficient than they are so they can receive the effective input they need.

We all must be active participants in these kinds of advocacies so that the multiple perception of minority children will come to an end. When the first-language and second-language communities share their questions, their answers, their frustrations, and their joys with one another, a new respect for minority children can be forged. A respect born of understanding. A respect born of knowledge. A respect born of knowing what it is like to view the world from a child's perspective: fun, interesting, challenging, frustrating, and sometimes frightening. By working together, we will all know what it means to grow for a living.

## References

Aaronson, E., N. Bloney, C. Stephan, J. Sikes, and M. Snapp. 1978. *The Jigsaw Classroom*. Beverly Hills, Calif.: Sage.

Bereiter, C., and S. Englemann. 1966. *Teaching Disadvantaged Children in the Preschool*. Englewood Cliffs, N.J.: Prentice-Hall.

Calkins, L. 1983. *Lessons from a Child*. Exeter, N.H.: Heinemann.

Cummins, J. 1981. The Role of Primary Language Development in Promoting Educational Success for Language Minority Students. In *Schooling and Language Minority Students: A Theoretical Framework*, Office of Bilingual Bicultural Education, 3–49. Los Angeles: California State University, Evaluation, Dissemination, and Assessment Center.

Edelsky, C. 1986. *Writing in a Bilingual Program: Había una Vez*. Norwood, N.J.: Ablex.

Enright, D. S., and M. L. McCloskey. 1985. Yes, Talking! Organizing the Classroom to Promote Second Language Acquisition. *TESOL Quarterly* 19 (3): 431–53.

Goodman, K. 1967. Reading: A Psycholinguistic Guessing Game. *Journal of the Reading Specialist* 4:126–35.

Goodman, Y., and C. Burke. 1972. *The Reading Miscue Inventory*. New York: Macmillan. (2d ed. from Richard C. Owen Publishers, New York.)

Graves, D. 1983. *Writing: Teachers and Children at Work*. Exeter, N.H.: Heinemann.

Harste, J. D., V. Woodward, and C. Burke. 1984. *Language Stories and Literacy Lessons*. Portsmouth, N.H.: Heinemann.

Hudelson, S. 1984. Kan Yu Ret an Rayt en Ingles: Children Become Literate in ESL. *TESOL Quarterly* 18 (2): 221–38.

————. 1985. *Hopscotch*. Englewood Cliffs, N.J.: Prentice-Hall.

————. 1986. ESL Children's Writing: What We've Learned; What We're Learning. In *Children and ESL: Integrating Perspectives*, edited by P. Rigg and D. S. Enright. Washington, D.C.: TESOL.

Hudelson, S., ed. 1981. *Learning to Read in Different Languages*. Washington, D.C.: Center for Applied Linguistics.

Krashen, S. D. 1982. *Principles and Practices in Second Language Acquisition*. Hayward, Calif.: Alemany/Janus.

Kreeft, J., R. Shuy, J. Staton, L. Reed, and R. Morroy. 1984. *Dialogue Writing: Analysis of Student-Teacher Interactive Writing in the Learning of English as a Second Language*. Final report, National Institute of Education, Grant No. NIE-G-83-0030. Washington, D.C.: Georgetown University Press, #ED 252097.

Kuhn, T. 1962. *The Structure of Scientific Revolution*. Chicago: University of Chicago Press.

Rigg, P. 1986. Reading in ESL: Learning from Kids. In *Children and ESL: Integrating Perspectives*, edited by P. Rigg and D. S. Enright. Washington, D.C.: TESOL.

Sarton, M. 1973. *Journal of a Solitude*. New York: W. W. Norton.

Smith, F. 1983. Afterthoughts. *Essays into Literacy*. Portsmouth, N.H.: Heinemann.

————. 1985. *Reading without Nonsense*. New York: Teachers College.

Snow, C. 1977. Mothers' Speech Research: From Input to Interaction. In *Talking to Children*, edited by C. Snow and C. Ferguson. New York: Cambridge University Press.

Urzúa, C. 1977–78. Unpublished personal observations of a kindergarten classroom in Austin, Texas.

————. 1981. *Speak with a Purpose*. Skokie, Ill.: National Textbook.

————. 1987. "You Stopped Too Soon": Second Language Children Composing and Revising. *TESOL Quarterly* 21 (2): 279–304.

Wells, C. G. 1981. *Learning through Instruction: The Study of Language Development*. Cambridge: Cambridge University Press.

# 3 The Classroom: A Good Environment for Language Learning

Judith Wells Lindfors
University of Texas, Austin

It's an interesting paradox that the more we find out about how language development differs from individual to individual and situation to situation, the more we find out about how it is similar for all. The specific differences shed light on and help us identify the deep general and unifying principles that operate across those specific differences of individual learners and situations. The first given is this: virtually all children effortlessly and naturally learn their native tongue, and many learn at least one more language as well. The second given is this: the specific situations in which this effortless learning occurs are very different one from another. The question, then, is this: how does it happen that the same result—the ability to communicate effectively in at least one language—is achieved through such diversity? The answer involves two parts: (1) what is *there*—the environment—for the child to use, and (2) the ways that the child uses it. Of course, these turn out to be the two most fundamental interests of the classroom teacher: providing a rich learning environment for children and supporting them in their effective use of it.

Though language development continues throughout life, it is most dramatic in the early years, before the child comes to school. An initial look at the environments in which young children develop their language reveals a great deal of variety. Children learn the language(s) of their social group, whatever the physical conditions, political systems, economic circumstances, cultural orientation, etc., of that group. And whatever the group's family structures, religious beliefs, moral values, educational practices, and social mores, the children learn the language(s). But even within the experience of any particular child the variation in language experience seems extraordinary: the child encounters language used for many different communication purposes (e.g., explaining, coaxing, promising, inviting, entertaining, deceiving), in many different types of events (conversations, rock songs, storybooks, scoldings, letters from grandma), involving many different participants and focusing on many different topics. The variety in every child's language world is quite remarkable.

However, a closer look reveals a crucial commonality: namely, that the specific language situations children in any society encounter are all real communication events. That is, people are engaging in the events in order to communicate with one another, *not* in order to "teach" the child his or her language. No, they're not "teaching" language, they're *doing* language—joking, informing, arguing, inquiring, comforting, challenging, and so on. The fact that the child learns language from the pervasive absence of explicit instruction has led some people to refer to language learning as "learning without teaching." The fact is that across an incredible array of specific environmental differences, there is one stunning commonality: it is *living* language that the child's environment is full of, language *in use*, communication.

It's quite incredible that, with people all around using language with her and with each other but not explicitly trying to teach her language, the child gets language figured out—language, that incredibly complex and abstract system for relating meanings (what we express) and expression (the ways we convey meanings). This brings us to our second question, the question of *how*: how does the child figure language out in this communication environment? What does the child *do* with what is *there*? We now know that the child does not try to take in and store specifics. Rather, he attends to the language around him in a selective way, tuning into it, noticing regularities and patterns that enable him to construct the organizational system that the talk and writing he encounters are examples of. The child— every child—is born to do this: to make *sense* of this mess of communication all around; to construct sense, order, design, organization. We do not hand a child our adult sense of language; the sense the child builds of language is his or her own, fashioned out of his or her own personal experience in the world. Many call the child's active sense-making "creative construction," "construction" in that it is the child's building of a system, and "creative" in that it is a system never explicitly given or described or taught, but rather a system fashioned by the child out of available, ever-present language material. It is a system gleaned, constructed, tried out, and confirmed in the many contexts of ongoing experience in the world, especially encounters with cognitive and social meanings and people's expression of them.

The child is well endowed for creatively constructing the language system that underlies the wide variety of bits and pieces she hears and sees. It is a human thing to do; it is, in fact, inevitable for a human to do this. Evolution has seen to this. Evolution has endowed our species, and no other, with unique anatomical and neurological mechanisms that we put to good use in figuring out how meaning and expression (signs, speech, written symbols) relate to one another and how to accomplish our many social purposes.

Yet it's easy to see that what is common for all in language learning—the child's creative construction process at work in her world of meaningful communication—is, at the same time, absolutely unique. For each human being, both the totality of personal experience (the "what is there") *and* his own active sense-making (his creative construction of language) will be his own, different from every other human's. The wonder of language! And of humans!

We see endless examples of children creatively constructing language out of their experience, if we know to look at children's language behavior—their talk and writing and reading—in this way. Here are some examples.[1]

- A five-year-old monolingual child is telling her mother a story for the wordless book *Hiccup*.

  > The drink accidently got on her, and she was mad at him. But she forgived him . . . The girl, the girl hippopotamus was eating a sandwich and the boy was eating a ham—uh—a apple. And they were both hiccuping. And they both hiccuping and hiccuping and hiccuping and they thought it was alicious. And they hollered at each other and they keeped on hiccuping . . . And she kicked him into the water. And she was alaughin' at him, and sticked her tongue out at him.

- A teacher asked a four-year-old monolingual child who was sweeping the nursery school floor, "Are you mopping?" The child replied, "No, I'm brooming."

- A four-year-old monolingual child had found one shoe and asked his father, "Where's the other shoe that rhymes with this one?"

- A Spanish-dominant kindergarten child "reads" *The Little Engine That Could* aloud: "El choo-choo train think I can. Once a choo-choo train so happy. Oso, [bear] and elephant, two dolly and own-uh-own [orange], apple, milk, candy. Said, 'Why you stop?'

'Wait, wait . . .' 'Wha happen?' 'You help us?' 'No, I tired for that. I too tired for that.' 'Stop! Stop! Stop!'

'Stop!' 'Wha happen?' 'The engine broke. Can you help us?' 'I, I, no, I too little. I think. . . all right, I can. Think I can, think I can, think I can, think I can, and then I can, and then I can, can, caaaaaaaan, (child is singing softly). 'I think I can, can, can. Now.' The end" (Seawell 1985, 127–28).

- A Spanish-dominant child, in second grade, starts her five-page story as seen in Figure 1.
- Monolingual Julia, five years old, is asked to write a letter and a song. Her work is reproduced in Figure 2.

You can see that these expressions are not the result of instruction or of imitation, because adult speakers of English would not have expressed themselves in these ways or taught anyone else to. You can also see that the children in these examples have figured out a great deal about how language works, and they are using that knowledge to guide their expression of their meanings as they communicate with others. Notice that these examples come from first- and second-language children, and they involve oral expression and written, but they all tell the same story: the tale of an active and creative sense-maker building an organizational system for communication even as she participates actively in communication, the very phenomenon she is figuring out.

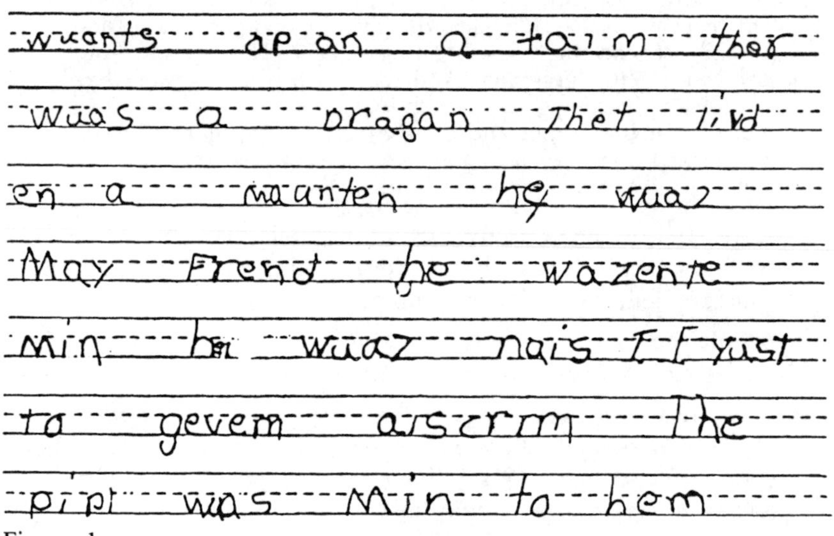

Figure 1

Figure 2

No one is more concerned than the classroom teacher with the "what is there" in the child's learning environment and with supporting the use the child makes of it. That's simply the business of being a teacher. It's comforting to know that, in terms of children's language development in classroom settings, what's good for the first-language learner is good for the second: Children develop language best by observing and engaging in authentic communication—language used in situations that are meaningful and purposeful to participants. And so it is of crucial importance to recognize what is, and is not, authentic communication.

Interestingly, when we reflect on particular possible scenarios involving words outside of the classroom, we recognize quite easily which are authentic and which are not. Consider some examples.

- If you came into my kitchen at breakfast time, you would find each family member reading a different section of the morning paper while eating. And if one of us suddenly said, "Now *here's* a guy with a problem. 'Dear Abby . . .' " and continued to read the humorous letter aloud, this would not strike you as strange. But if you came in and found us all looking at our individual copies of the same page of the newspaper and taking turns reading paragraphs of the same article aloud, one by one around the breakfast table, while the others listened and read along silently, this would strike you as odd. This is not what people do with newspapers. What they do with newspapers is find out things—what their horoscope says, what the weather's going to be, what Snoopy's up to, how the Red Sox did, who's having a sale on summer sandals.

- If you were having dinner with your eight-year-old nephew and his mother asked the child, "Have you seen Jonathan yet and asked him to your party?" you'd hardly notice. But if his mother asked him, "What can you tell me about this salt shaker?" you'd wonder why she was doing this. Language is for telling people things they want to know or things you want them to know. Language isn't for performing your ability to list attributes of salt shakers. Nobody wants to know that, and anyway, they can see for themselves.

- If you and I were in my car on our way to my home and we got completely stuck in rush-hour traffic and, while sitting there, I nudged the car forward a little so I could read the bumper sticker on the car in front of me—"If you can read this you're too close"—you'd think my behavior perfectly normal. But if, as we sat there, I whipped a set of flashcards out of my purse and started reading each one in my announcement voice—*can, close, if, too, this*—you'd think me strange. (Stranger still if I started giving definitions for each one.) Bumper stickers and flashcards look alike, but bumper stickers are language and flashcards aren't. Bumper stickers tell people things: they make jokes or tell what causes the driver supports or who he's voting for or where his kids go to college. But why would I "read" words that don't have any message for me? Language is for messages.

- If you found me sitting at my desk filling in the blanks on a catalog order form, you'd hardly notice. But if you found me sitting there selecting words with short vowel sounds from a list and writing them in the blanks in a set of unrelated sentences, you'd think this peculiar. Language is for doing things, like ordering socks and underwear. Order forms do things. So do some other kinds of fill-in-the-blank forms: income tax forms and crossword puzzles and lottery tickets. But not vowel exercises.

- You might find me sitting at my desk writing a letter. "Whatcha doing?" you'd ask. "Just dropping my sister a line to let her know our exact arrival time, now that our flight arrangements are finally definite." Of course. But what if, instead of this, I answered your question by saying, "I'm just dropping my sister a line using this set of spelling words" (showing you a set of ten *ie/ei* words). You'd think me either joking or mad. We write letters to tell people things, not to use a particular set of words.

It's easy enough to see which of these examples are really language—meaningful and purposeful—and which are not; easy enough to see which are authentic.[2] But when we're in the classroom, the distinction isn't always so easy. So much that is *in*authentic—*non*language—has for so long been accepted as what-people-do-in-school that the *in*authentic has taken on a life of its own. And so it seems perfectly reasonable for a teacher to have children read aloud around the circle from the same basal text, or to ask students questions she already knows the answer to in order to elicit a series of attributes that are visible to all present, or to have students "read" words on flashcards or fill in blanks on worksheets or write text "using as many of this week's spelling words as you can." This isn't language outside of the classroom, and it isn't language inside the classroom either. Children develop language by doing language, not by doing something else.

## Making the Classroom Authentic

The good news is that classrooms can be—and many are—authentic language environments for children to creatively construct their first and second languages in. I choose to demonstrate this with three examples, one which primarily involves reading, and one which primarily involves writing. I say "primarily" here because authentic communication usually involves more than one way of using language. For example, if you liked reading the book, you'll probably go see the movie; if your friend writes to you, you'll probably write back (or maybe call); I tend, while talking (listening) on the phone, to jot down topics I want to be sure my friend and I "cover" before we hang up. However much we talk about "speaking," "listening," "reading," and "writing" as if they were separate and distinct, they aren't, of course; they're all tangled up in our real experience, and so they should be. And so my "oral" example is only partly that: it begins as somebody's talk but immediately is somebody's listening, and who knows what writing and reading events it might lead to. And so with my "reading" and "writing" examples. They're really much more. I choose my examples from the only possible starting place: children and experiences I know they love, for these are bound to be authentic.

In the first class I ever taught, second grade, my children used to tell me what they liked and didn't like by using the phrases *get to* or *have to,* as in "Do we have to do X today?" (You can hear the different tones of voice, can't you?)

## Show and Tell

One of the absolutely predictable daily "get to's" was "show and tell." I confess I never could understand why. What, I wondered, could be so compelling about telling or listening to others tell about an object or event that, from my perspective at least, was often minimally interesting at best. But we had show and tell almost daily, not because I understood why the children liked it, and not because I saw special value in it, but basically because there were twenty-four of them and only one of me. But now I'm glad they outnumbered me, and I see that they were right. The situation was authentic: they wanted to tell each other about the events and objects they lugged in; they wanted to have and to be audiences for one another. And I'm sure there were matters of social status and acceptance and such which were crucial here that I didn't even begin to recognize. But these are language, too—what language is about, what language is for. So show and tell was authentic for these children, and it was a "get to" *because* it was authentic for them. But besides this, it was the perfect opportunity for them to control,[3] to shape, to design— yes, to creatively construct both what to tell and how. And their response to classmates' tellings were of their own constructing, too.

I see now that the children and I could have carried this much further. We could have had the day's show-ers and tellers set themselves up in different areas of the classroom. Each would have needed enough space to demonstrate what his or her object could do and to allow other children to try it out. Classmates of the show-ers and tellers could have moved freely from one area to another according to their particular interests. Or we might have extended this display-type format into a "show-and-tell fair" and invited another class to come and visit. Or we might have sometimes broken into smaller groups so that each child could have had more opportunities to show/tell and so that the interaction could have been more conversational and less performance-like. "Author's chair" (Calkins 1986) seems a particularly rich variation of the basic show-and-tell idea: the child author reads aloud to his classmates what he has written and invites input and discussion from them. There were many possibilities, but I didn't see them then. Show and tell seemed to me so marginal, even trivial. I thought we had more important things to do. I was wrong.

I also see now the special value that this experience would hold for the ESL child. It would have provided the perfect situation for the child to participate in socially, the first concern of the second-language learner. It would have provided contextual support that could have helped the child to convey his or her meanings and to grasp those expressed by others. Above all, it would have provided a real reason for the child to interact with classmates and to shape his or her own message in his or her own way in the new language.

*Story Time*

Another good thing we had going, a "get to" for my second graders, was story time. Now this one is as old as humankind. We were never more engaged together—all of us—than when I read *Charlotte's Web* or some other favorite aloud. But if this was so good (and we all knew it was), more would have been even better. And, as I see it now, I could have done so much more. I could have varied the tales, the tellers, the audiences, and the ways of the tellings (the presentations) in many ways.

1. *The tales.* Besides favorite children's books to read aloud, I could have used:

   • wordless storybooks for which the children would have provided verbal texts.

   • ongoing classroom events written in a classroom journal or in a class newspaper that would have circulated through the school and to the children's homes regularly.

   • dramas created spontaneously in the sociodramatic area of the classroom.

   • favorite stories played, or new ones created, in the puppet area of the classroom—real episodes from my own experience (I find that many children are fascinated with the personal incidents their teachers tell).

   • comics read and sometimes created by the children.

   • narrative songs and poems.

   • the children's own written narratives on topics, real or imagined, that they had selected themselves.

   • picture stories. I think immediately of Polaroid pictures the children might have taken while on a walk, to which they later could have added text to make a picture story. I also think of the ongoing pictures and text some kindergarten children provided over several weeks as they observed eggs and then newly hatched chicks and a caterpillar that finally became a butterfly.

- biography. Some fine published biographies are available, but autobiography also could have been an important type of writing and telling for the children. Older children could have been helpful scribe-partners for many students who could have told their life stories for the older children to write down for them. (See Tassell 1983 for a description of such a partnering autobiographical project.)

- the child's own ongoing personal journal or diary (written or taped).

- plays to be read or written.

- oral histories. I think of some school children whose study of the Depression era included interviewing older people in their neighborhoods to gather oral histories of their experience during the Depression.

2. *The tellers.* Besides myself, I could have drawn on:

- adults whom I and the children could have invited to come into the classroom to read aloud (e.g., school personnel, parents, community folks, children from upper grades, especially the children's heroes). My students could have decided whom they wanted and then invited them to come. Especially fascinating would have been readers with various voices and dialects and styles—a variety that might have been interestingly demonstrated by having several different people read the same story to the children.

- professionals on record or on tape.

- the children themselves, reading their own narratives they had written, or choosing and reading favorite stories to classes of younger children.

3. *The audiences.* I tended to think always of the whole class listening together as I read aloud. But I could also have thought of:

- an individual child at the listening center.

- pairs of children in a quiet corner—classmates, perhaps, or maybe cross-grade partners—reading or telling stories to one another.
- small groups at a listening center, following a taped story together in their accompanying books.
- me as audience. Every time a child came to me with, "Know what?" and I answered, "No, what?" I had accepted the audience role, just as I did when I listened and responded to the child as she read something to me that she had written.

4. *The ways of telling.* I thought mainly of myself reading aloud, but I rarely thought of:

- a telling instead of a reading.
- the tape-recorded voice.
- dramatization the children using their own voices and bodies to express sequences of events.
- dramatization through the use of puppets.
- the professional's voice on tape or record.
- the children's own dramatization recorded and presented on videotape.

And we mustn't forget the most basic of all: the child sitting down with a book and as much time as he wants to read it. All these would have provided ways for the children to creatively construct meaning and expression in and through story, the most timelessly and universally authentic event of all.

## Dialogue Journals

Dialogue journals are my third example.[4] People sometimes talk about dialogue journals as if they were new, but they're not. Only the label is new. The event itself is far older than we are: it's people who want to write to each other doing just that, and writing about what they want to write about and responding to each other's writing. That's surely a "get to."

Recently I did a month of dialogue-journal writing with a class of Zulu sixth grade students (ages twelve to sixteen) in South Africa. The students' writing gave me a new appreciation for creative construction in authentic communication contexts. At the beginning, one student wrote, "I'll write to you . . . I want to communicate." And that's what we did. The students expressed a wide range of communication purposes in their writing.

- They used the writing *to teach*. For example, several gave me lessons in Zulu—lists of Zulu words and sentences along with their English translations.

- They used their writing *to inquire*. One girl asked,

  Does American children at the age like me have a boyfriend? If they have them, does they show them to their parents like TV shows us?

- They used their writing *to joke*, as in

  Thabiso says to his teacher, Sir, would you beat a boy for something he did not do?
  Teacher: Of course not Thabiso.
  Thabiso: That's good sir, I don't do my homework.

- And they used their writing *to inform*. One student wrote,

  When you visit at Town most of people they go on Saturdays because haven't got no time because during the other days they worked.

  When we go to town let me say you go with boyfriend to visit somewhere at town when you finish to buy grocery we visit at byeskop or museum we walk very nice because we are free.

- They used written English *to scold* as in the following example, in which a student scolded me for not being quick enough in getting him a pen pal.

  Mrs. Lindfors you didn't answer me about a friend (girl) not a girlfriend. I want a person who will wrote for me and I wrote for her.

- And they used it *to offer*, as in:

  If is there any question that you do not understand send for me, I will be here to tell you.

  They used their journal writing *to request*. For example,

  If we finished to write on these journal can I take it from my home?

- They used this writing *to seek clarification*. I had asked one student to tell me about how teachers in South Africa help pupils to learn. He wrote back:

  I don't understand what do you mean about "What teachers here do to help the pupils."

- They also used it *to compliment*. One wrote,

I told my patness [partners] about Miss professor Lindfors. She is a beautifull lady, a short lady a funny lady. And I like him too much. She is clever women. She is a lovely lady. My classmates love him.

- They used their writing *to apologize.* For example,

I am very sorry to call you Judith because I don't no you surname. But I think you don't mind.

- They used written English *to explain.* One wrote,

I like to explain what's a play mother. Is a girl whom you see every time and you seem to love her or is she who loves you. She will like you to be her baby but not really one and she is your play mother. Example: When I say to Brenda that I love her to be my mother. You know that I'm not her really child . . . It's just a game isn't true. In Zulu we say *umama wokudlala. Dladla* means play. *Mama* means mother.

- And they used this writing *to express opinions.* For example,

I like this teacher. Oh! She's a good teacher. I think the principal's must promote her.

- And they used their free writing *to make conversation comments.*

Just look how many pages did we write now.

And

Bye-bye. Have a nice weekend reading *True Love.*

- They used written English *to express thanks.* One wrote,

Thanks you said to be patient, be patient b_____ Thanks I will be patient

- One student used the writing *to comfort.*

Some of my classmates told me that you have asked him that are you safe here in South Africa. I say Don't be worry, you are safe from *amabutho*, because now we are protected . . . So don't be worry.

- And several used their writing *to reflect.*

I tried many ways to have a friend who is a European who lives in South Africa. But they concerd [consider?] us as nothing. They say that we don't know nothing. But type of people doesn't matter. The matter is that how do you trust each other.

Did you believe that God is a King of the world? Many people said that God is not a king and Bible is same like a story. He [I] beleive that God is a king and Bible is a true.

- Besides writing for their own purposes, these students wrote on their own topics:

> If you want to be good in karate you must respect your treiner and do all what he/she tell you. When I was new in karate, the treiner asked me to fight with a girl. The girl kick me on the face and hit me on the chest. When i saw that things are bad, I ran away and everybody laughed at me they said "you are not a brave boy instaed you are the coward boy." When they have laughed at me I was shy.

> Sorry, Judith today I want to tell you about a poor people live in Topiya [Ethiopia] That people are very poor and I see in TV and Pacebook thay have no place to sleep and they have no food to eat they become small children and parents of those children I think you are very sorry for this people and I very sorry for this country.

> In our school we [have] a child his name is F_____. When is cold she is wearing a jersey which collar is hair of sheep which light brown. She is naught and noise when she laugh she make a noise . . . When she is sit she open the mouth everyday, teachers tell her. "Close the mouth, F_____" and close the mouth. She is 13 years old. She a dirty she clean only day she like to be clean.

> I want to tell you about my party. my party was at night on July 30 Its start on a.m. 9.30 up to 1:00 a.m. My mother gave me new dress and she bought a cake, drinks, delicious food my mother cook those food I tell my friends about my party and I take many photograph for my party You like my party? "Judith."

In their dialogue journals these students were creatively constructing their second language. They were forging ways to express their own meanings so that I could understand and respond to them. *Respond*, not correct; respond with meanings and expression of my own. B_____ writes to me still. In a letter he sent about six months after I had left South Africa he wrote:

> "Here a secret" One day I was coming from school and I was a lot of work to do and I sit down and rest and I had a call that call was coming from M_____ [a friend of B_____'s from the dialogue-journal writing class, no longer attending the same school as B_____] did you wrote Mr Lindfors, "B_____ [said] Oh yes my friend I write to her every month. And after we finished our talking I went to my bedroom, What I am looking for? "I ask myself" I am looking for the small journal which I was used last year at school. And I found at last but I was very happy to find it. And I read day and day.

Dialogue-journal writing was a "get to" for B_____. It was, and remains, authentic.

The message is clear enough: children's development of language (first or second) is fostered in classroom communication situations that are purposeful to the child and that engage her in creatively constructing language for herself. We can, of course, ignore this. But if we choose to take it seriously, show and tell, stories, and dialogue journals are good places to begin.

## Acknowledgments

Portions of this chapter previously appeared in these publications:

Judith W. Lindfors, *Children's Language and Learning*, 2/E, © 1987, pp. 3, 77, 160, 161, 162, 360–362, 452. Reprinted by permission of Prentice-Hall, Inc., Englewood Cliffs, N.J.

From "Exploring in and through Language" by Judith W. Lindfors, 1983, *TESOL '82: Pacific Perspectives on Language Learning and Teaching.* Adapted by permission.

## Notes

1. These examples also occur in Lindfors 1987. I thank Judy Muery, Janet Rothschild, John Henderson, Pat Seawell, Sarah Hudelson, and Judith King for them.

2. The term *authentic* is Edelsky and Draper's. For an insightful and provocative discussion of authenticity and inauthenticity in classrooms, see their article, "Reading/'Reading,' Writing/'Writing,' Text/'Text'."

3. Sarah Michaels's work on sharing-time suggests that, in fact, the teacher (myself in this case) controls this event more than she thinks she does. See, for example, Michaels and Collins 1984.

4. See *Dialogue*, a newsletter from the Center for Applied Linguistics, for descriptions of ways that classroom teachers have been using dialogue journals with first- and second-language learners.

## References

Calkins, L. M. 1986. *The Art of Teaching Writing.* Portsmouth, N.H.: Heinemann.

Edelsky, C., and K. Draper. In Press. Reading/'Reading,' Writing/'Writing,' Text/'Text.' In *Reading and Writing: Theory and Research*, edited by A. Petrosky. Norwood, N.J.: Ablex.

Lindfors, J. W. 1983. Exploring in and through Language. In *On TESOL '82: Pacific Perspectives on Language Learning and Teaching*, edited by M. Clarke and J. Handscombe. Washington, D.C.: TESOL.

———. 1987. *Children's Language and Learning.* 2d ed. Englewood Cliffs, N.J.: Prentice-Hall.

Michaels, S., and J. Collins. 1984. Oral Discourse Styles: Classroom Inter-
    action and the Acquisition of Literacy. In *Coherence in Spoken and Written
    Discourse*, edited by D. Tannen. Norwood, N.J.: Ablex.

Seawell, R. P. M. 1985. A Micro-Ethnographic Study of a Spanish/English
    Bilingual Kindergarten in which Literature and Puppet Play Were Used
    as a Method of Enhancing Language Growth. Doctoral dissertation,
    University of Texas at Austin.

Tassell, F. V. 1983. A Writing Assignment with a Different Flair. *Language
    Arts* 60 (3): 354–56.

# 4 Literature as a Support to Language Acquisition

Virginia G. Allen
The Ohio State University

Pornsith, a ten-year-old Laotian boy, was observed for more than two weeks in a school setting. The child had been in the school less than one year. Most of his day was spent in a mainstream classroom where he was the only second-language learner. The observer, a graduate student, spent mornings in the school, watching and listening to the child in a variety of settings to see how he was attending to and using language. During the ten days she spent in the classroom, she found that the child used language very little. He seldom communicated with other children, and when he did, it was by the use of nods, smiles, and gestures. During the entire observation period, the only talking that Pornsith did in class was in response to the teacher's daily question, "What are you doing for lunch?" When the teacher talked to the whole class, Pornsith did not appear to be attending.

Twice a week Pornsith met with the special reading teacher who worked with him alone on tasks taken from the basal reading series. The following observation was made during one of those sessions.

*Teacher:* OK. We're going to do rhyming words today. (She takes out a large stack of colorful pictures with words printed below each picture.)

*Pornsith:* Who draw these pictures?

*Teacher:* I did. (She smiles at him.)

*Pornsith:* Oh. (He smiles back at her and continues to look through the pictures.)

*Teacher:* Let's see if you can tell me what each of these are. (She picks up a picture of a box and hands it to him.) Do you know what this is?

*Pornsith:* Bock.

*Teacher:* OK. It's a box. (She emphasizes the ending sound.)

*Pornsith:* Box.

*Teacher:* Good.

*Pornsith:* (Points to another picture.) What's that?
*Teacher:* That's snow. Can you say that? Snow.
*Pornsith:* Snow.
*Teacher:* Very good.
*Pornsith:* (Picks up a picture.) Can I have this?
*Teacher:* Well, I need it to show to the other children. (She smiles at him.)
*Pornsith:* Oh. (He smiles back.)

Toward the end of her two-week stay in the classroom, the observer read the story *The Gingerbread Boy* (Galdone 1975) to Pornsith. She noted that he followed the pictures with great interest and chuckled at various parts of the story. Occasionally, he would reach over to point at a detail in one of the illustrations. Following the reading she asked him about the story.

*Observer:* What happened at the beginning of the story?
*Pornsith:* He can shrink . . . and . . . and . . . the fock eat.
*Observer:* What about the old man and the old woman? What did they do?
*Pornsith:* He can't get him.
*Observer:* Who else was trying to get him?
*Pornsith:* The fock.
*Observer:* Were there any other animals?
*Pornsith:* Bear, cow . . . and . . .
*Observer:* And what did they all try to do?
*Pornsith:* And the fock eat.
*Observer:* What happened when the fox was in the river? In the water?
*Pornsith:* He swim.
*Observer:* Where was the gingerbread boy?
*Pornsith:* On the stomach.
*Observer:* The water was getting deeper and deeper. What did the fox tell him to do?
*Pornsith:* (With enthusiasm and gestures.) C'mon my head!
*Observer:* And then the water got even deeper. What did the fox say?
*Pornsith:* C'mon my nose! (Points to his own nose.)
*Observer:* And then what happened?
*Pornsith:* C'mon my mouth! (His voice rises and he opens his mouth wide and points inside.)
*Observer:* He opened his big mouth and . . .
*Pornsith:* Yeah.
*Observer:* And he . . .
*Pornsith:* Ate!

*Observer:* What did the gingerbread boy say to everybody who was trying to catch him?

*Pornsith:* Everybody no catch me!

*Observer:* Why did the old woman make a gingerbread boy?

*Pornsith:* It's a cake.

*Observer:* How come no one could eat him?

*Pornsith:* (Chuckling.) Because no catch him.

*Observer:* And who finally caught him?

*Pornsith:* The fock!

The language that occurred in each of the three settings was very different. In the classroom, where the teacher directed almost all of her talk to the whole group, Pornsith did not seem to have any expectation that he could make sense out of most of the language that swirled about him. He survived by watching other children and, when possible, following their lead. Pornsith obviously enjoyed the undivided attention of the reading teacher. The pictures helped clarify meaning for him and allowed him to respond. The nature of the talk, however, tended to limit his responses to one word. But in the third situation, Pornsith not only showed a lively interest in the story and in retelling it, he also demonstrated a much greater ability to both understand and to produce language than might have been expected.

Pornsith was clearly supported by the story. The book, *The Gingerbread Boy,* presented him with a large, cohesive, uninterrupted chunk of language. The story was made comprehensible by strong illustrations, patterned and repetitive language, and a predictable story structure. Pornsith expected the story to make sense. He was clearly focused on meaning. Repeated patterns allowed him to begin to match his language with the language of the text. Even with his limited command of English, Pornsith was able to reconstruct the story. The support of this patterned predictable text, coupled with strong illustrations, not only helped the child to build proficiencies in listening and speaking, but also helped him to begin to take on the reader's role.

All children need to have opportunities to hear the language of stories and to explore beautifully illustrated books. Sharing storybooks with children is too frequently viewed simply as a pleasurable break in the school day: a nice way to rest after recess, a way to fill in time before the bell rings, something teachers do for young children but unnecessary in upper grade classrooms. Yet research shows that reading aloud to children has a significant effect not only on literacy acquisition (Durkin 1966; Clark 1976), but also on language development (Chomsky 1972; Wells 1986). For the child who is acquiring English as a second language, this literacy input is vital. English-as-a-second-language programs that emphasize skills and workbook activities can deprive these young language learners of the richly supportive context offered by good children's books.

In selecting books to share with the second-language learner, the teacher needs to consider illustration. The illustrator plays a significant role in helping the child attach meaning to the text. Basal reader systems, which more and more frequently are attempting to include selections from children's literature by good authors, often do not use the illustrations that are a part of these books. If they do, frequently the placement and size are changed to accommodate the format of the reading book. The dimensions of a good picture book are an important part of its message. The width of the double-page spread in *The Ox-Cart Man* (Hall 1979) allows the illustrator, Barbara Cooney, not only to show the path of the ox-cart man's journey, but to create a sense of the length of that trip. The dramatic appearance of the huge paw of the lion in Martin and Young's *Foolish Rabbit's Big Mistake* (1985), creates a sense of the frightening power of the king of beasts in ways that words alone could not.

The illustrations found in concept books link words to their meanings with immediacy and force. Hoban's *Push, Pull, Empty, Full* (1971) with its clear, uncluttered photography makes explicit the meanings of opposites. *Empty* and *full* are illustrated by gumball machines while *in* and *out* are demonstrated by an obliging turtle. Peter Spier's *People* (1980) explores the many cultural facets of such words as *beauty, play*, and *home*. Myriads of detailed drawings illustrate how such concepts vary from culture to culture. Illustrations, however, can do more than depict the literal meaning of a text. The best illustrations extend the text and can help children get at underlying meaning. In the book *I Have a Friend*, Narashi (1987) recounts all the things that one little boy's friend can do, such as sliding down steps, stretching to reach the treetops, and keeping secrets safe. Only the pictures tell us that the friend is a shadow. In the cumulative text *The Napping House*, by Audrey and Don Wood (1984), the pictures let us follow the text, which tells of how first a child, then a dog, then a cat, then a mouse, and finally a flea all pile into the bed of a "snoring granny." Additionally, the changing perspectives and changing light in the illustrations create a sense of movement through both space and time. Even a child whose English is still limited can begin to discover that reading is much more than getting the meaning of individual words; it involves the interaction of the reader with the book.

Language must be carefully considered in selecting books for the language-different child. This does not mean that texts need to be "made easy" by limiting the length of sentences, the number of words within the text, or the number of syllables in words. Rather, texts should support meaning by being predictable. A book with a repetitive refrain, such as Pat Hutchins's *The Doorbell Rang* (1986), will simply invite children to pick up the refrain and chorus, "Nobody bakes cookies like Grandma!" Folktales, with their conventional beginnings and endings and reoccurring characters and form, help children to predict both the actions and the language of the story. Such texts give second-language learners pieces of language with which to play and to experiment. One Cambodian child had heard a number of times Sendak's poem, *Chicken Soup with Rice* (1982), with its refrain, "Sipping once, sipping twice, sipping chicken soup with rice." On the playground one snowy day the child took a spill on an icy patch. He looked up at his teacher and grinned and said, "Slipping once, slipping twice, slipping on the slippy ice!"

Books can do more than provide an input of vocabulary and structure. They can give children something to talk about by providing a very special kind of shared experience. Books allow for comparisons and contrasts and can be grouped in a number of ways. For example, children can explore books by one author, books focused on a theme, or different versions of one tale. A teacher observed one group of Southeast Asian students having a heated discussion in the reading corner. These girls had several versions of *Cinderella* spread out on the floor. They were moving back and forth between the books and looking at the pictures with much attention. As the teacher listened in, she heard them working hard to decide in which book Cinderella wore the most beautiful dress, in which book was the prince the handsomest, and in which was the stepmother the ugliest. No ESL lesson on the construction of the comparative and the superlative could have provided such enthusiastic and extensive practice!

Shared books can be extended in ways that permit children to use language for a variety of functions. One group of second-language learners had enjoyed the book *Jumanji* (Van Allsburg 1981), a picture book fantasy which focuses on a game that, when played, has some exotic and frightening consequences. These children decided to create their own game based on this book. They worked together planning the game, creating the board, and finally writing directions so that other children could also play their game. The first draft of their directions said:

> First you need one dice and you have to choose who is first by every one has to roll a dice who got the highest number get to be first. You need four marker It's is red yellow green blue marker If you roll the dice and then you move marker number space as the dice say. If land on a tree you drawn a card. the one who land on a gold city win you have to roll the exact number of spaces to get in the golden city.

Classmates were invited to play the game. When these players had some difficulty in understanding how they were to play the game, the rules were revised and tried again. The second version follows:

> First you need one dice and you have to choose who is first by everyone has to roll a dice.
> Who got the highest number gets to be first.
> You need four markers
> There are red, yellow, green, and blue markers.
> Start in the jungle.
> You roll the dice and then you move the marker the number of spaces as the dice say.
> If you land on a tree you draw a card. Read the card and do what it says.
> The one who lands on the Gold City wins.
> You have to roll the exact number of spaces to get in the Golden City.
> If you roll too high a number you stay in the same place until you do roll the exact number.
>
> Game designed by: Sithisom Nanthavongdouangsy
>                              Khenh Pouayvongsa
>                              Neuang Singhavong

The power of the book *Jumanji* created a link between these boys that sustained them as they talked about the book, extended the author's concept, and used writing to instruct the behavior of a new audience.

Well-selected books can be a model for writing by providing a framework that supports children as they move through a piece of writing. After looking at a variety of ABC books or counting books, children can create their own. Other types of books will provide a pattern that can be modified. *Brown Bear, Brown Bear* (Martin 1983) helped one group of children to create their own book, *Brown Bunny, Brown Bunny*, when a lop-eared rabbit became a member of their class. After reading a number of folktales that had magic objects in them, such as *Strega Nona, Jack and the Beanstalk, Akimba and the Magic*

*Cow,* and *Too Much Nose* to her ESL students, the teacher brought in a basket of "magic objects." Among the objects were a pair of old spectacles, a silver bracelet that looked like a serpent, a gold lace bonnet, and a quill pen. The children examined each object and discussed what magical properties it might have. All of these were listed on the board. The children then wrote their own magic object story. One ten-year-old boy wrote this story about the magic bracelet.

> Once upon a time there was a man named Kimball. He was the poorest man in his village. One day he went off to the woods. And dan Kimball saw old man planting crops. And Kimball helped the old man plant his crops. The old man was greatful that he told that there was magic blacelet behide the bush. And than Kimball went to the bush and saw a blacelet. The blacelet gives gold said the old man. And Kimball said thank you for magic blacelet. And then Kimball went home. And he live happily forever.

Not only did the sharing of folktales provide a form that supported this child as he wrote, it also gave him an input of literary language upon which he could draw. This influence can be seen in both sentence structure and in vocabulary.

Good literature for children can do more than help young second-language learners acquire the language of stories. If these boys and girls are to succeed in academic settings, they must be able to use print both to gain access to knowledge and to share their knowledge with others. An examination of textbooks in such areas of the curriculum as science, health, and social studies can prove these books to be very difficult for a child who does not share the native language of the writer of the text. Such textbooks are dense with information and specialized vocabulary. If they are the only source of information on a given topic, the non-native speaker is often denied access to information that the other children in the class are learning. However, there are numbers of superb informational books for children that can support second-language learners as they explore new domains. Children can gain a great deal of information about dinosaurs from such books as Aliki's *Digging Up Dinosaurs* (1987) and Emberly's *More Dinosaurs* (1983), even if they are not able to read the text. For older children, the marvels of the bones, blood vessels, sinews, and organs of the body are made clear in Miller's beautifully designed, three-dimensional book, *The Human Body* (1983). The movable illustrations allow them to put into action the valves of the heart and veins, to lift the rib cage to find the lungs, and to see how an image is projected onto the retina of the eye. While a textbook discussion of medieval history might be far too difficult for the second-language learner, books such as *Cathedral* (Macaulay 1973), *The Lutrell Village* (Sancha 1982), and *A Medieval Feast* (Aliki 1983) convey enormous amounts of information about the lifestyles and concerns of people who lived in those times by their meticulously detailed and accurate illustrations. While such books are a valuable resource for all children, they are a necessity for children who are still in the process of acquiring English.

However, it is not enough simply to make a rich array of children's books available. A literature program should be developed that includes all children, but should be designed in ways to provide special support to the second-language learner. The cornerstone of the program would be the reading aloud of books to children each day. Teachers whose classrooms include second-language learners should select with care the books they are sharing with the whole class, choosing ones that will help the child who is less proficient in English tap into the meaning.

There should also be time to share books with the non-native child by himself or herself, so that the child can talk through a book, ask questions, explore pictures, chime in, and read along. Parents who read aloud to their youngsters at home can attest to the fact that children love to hear the same storybook read over and over and yet over again. Second-language learners need to have the opportunity to hear familiar stories read again and again. The teacher is not the only one who can share books with children: other children in the class, older children, and parents can be readers as well. Once a book has been shared, it can be taped so that children can listen to it as often as they wish. There need to be opportunities for children to select books they want to read, and uninterrupted blocks of time for reading. Just as important is providing time for children to talk together about books and to share books they have enjoyed. Such talk not only deepens understandings, but provides a real purpose for oral language.

Topics of study need to be supported by a wide variety of strong books that invite children to explore and assist them to acquire new information and develop concepts. One important role of the teacher is to expand the breadth and depth of children's knowledge by making links between books. Finally, teachers need to watch and observe children as they listen to stories, talk about what they have heard and read, and extend books through art, talk, and writing. Children's response to books conveys to the observant teacher a great deal of information, not only about how children are taking on the structures and vocabulary of the new language, but how they are developing in their ability to get at meaning and to share their thinking.

## Acknowledgment

I thank Denise Visbal (M.A., The Ohio State University) for the samples of Pornsith's oral language.

## References

Aliki. 1983. *A Medieval Feast*. New York: Thomas Y. Crowell.

————. 1987. *Digging Up Dinosaurs*. New York: Harper and Row.

Cauley, L. B. 1989. *Jack and the Beanstalk*. New York: Putnam.

Chomsky, C. 1972. Stages in Language Development and Reading Exposure. *Harvard Educational Review* 42:1–33.

Clark, M. 1976. *Young Fluent Readers*. Portsmouth, N.H.: Heinemann.

De Paola, T. 1975. *Strega Nona*. Englewood Cliffs, N.J.: Prentice-Hall.

Durkin, D. 1966. *Children Who Read Early*. New York: Columbia Teachers College Press.

Emberly, M. 1983. *More Dinosaurs and Other Prehistoric Beasts*. Boston: Little, Brown.

Galdone, P. 1975. *The Gingerbread Boy*. Boston: Houghton Mifflin.

Hall, D. 1979. *The Ox-Cart Man*. Illustrated by B. Cooney. New York: Viking.

Hoban, T. 1971. *Push, Pull, Empty, Full: A Book of Opposites*. New York: Macmillan.

Hutchins, P. 1986. *The Doorbell Rang*. New York: Greenwillow.

Macaulay, D. 1973. *Cathedral*. Boston: Houghton Mifflin.

Martin, B., Jr. 1983. *Brown Bear, Brown Bear, What Do You See?* Illustrated by Eric Carle. New York: Holt.

————. 1985. *Foolish Rabbit's Big Mistake*. New York: Putnam.

Miller, J. 1983. *The Human Body*. Designed by D. Pelham. New York: Viking.

Narashi, K. 1987. *I Have a Friend*. New York: Atheneum.

Rose, A. 1976. *Akimba and the Magic Cow*. Illustrated by H. Merman. New York: Four Winds Press.

Sancha, S. 1982. *The Lutrell Village: Country Life in the Middle Ages*. New York: Thomas Y. Crowell.

Sendak, M. 1962. *Chicken Soup with Rice*. New York: Harper and Row.

Spier, P. 1980. *People*. New York: Doubleday.

Van Allsburg, C. 1981. *Jumanji*. Boston: Houghton Mifflin.

Wells, G. 1986. *The Meaning Makers: Children Learning Language and Using Language to Learn*. Portsmouth, N.H.: Heinemann.

Wood, A. 1984. *The Napping House*. Illustrated by D. Wood. New York: Harcourt, Brace, Jovanovich.

Zemach, H. 1967. *Too Much Nose: An Italian Tale*. Illustrated by M. Zemach. New York: Holt.

# 5 Language Experience Approach: Reading Naturally

Pat Rigg
American Language and Literacy, Tucson

In a first grade classroom in northern Arizona, the students—most of them Native Americans who speak Navajo as their first language— chant along with the teacher as she reads aloud, "Run, run, as fast as you can. You can't catch me, I'm the gingerbread man." When the clever fox has eaten the gingerbread man, the teacher asks the class, "Would you like me to write this story on the board so you can read it yourself?" "O!" (Navajo for "yes"), the kids agree. "OK, you decide what you want me to write, and when you're ready, tell me." In pairs and trios the students put their heads together and the room buzzes. After a few minutes of work together, the teacher asks for a volunteer to begin. "Once upon a time" a kid yells almost immediately, and the teacher writes that on the board. "Old woman and old man and little boy" offers another student, and the teacher writes that on the board, reads aloud, "Once upon a time old woman and old man and little boy," and waits for the next student's dictation.

This class is using the "Language Experience Approach" (LEA). The teacher is getting the students to dictate their own reading material. Because the Navajo word for *fox* is the same as their word for *coyote*, and because the coyote is the creator-trickster of many Navajo tales told in the winter months, this particular story is especially appealing to these Native American children on the reservation, combining as it does one of their favorite Navajo folk characters with the impudence of the childlike gingerbread man. And its appeal makes the story especially appropriate for conversion into LEA material.

In this chapter I want to (1) discuss why the Language Experience Approach is appropriate for students who are just learning to read English, (2) describe in some detail how to use the Language Experience Approach (LEA), and (3) address potential problems. Through-

out, I will refer to the students as **R**eaders and writers of **E**nglish as
**A**nother **L**anguage, or REAL students.

### Rationale

The main reason for using LEA with students who are just learning
to read in English is to involve the REAL students in creating their
own reading material. Teachers who have had many REAL students
know how difficult it is to find materials for the students to read.
First, the materials need to be interesting to the students, and that
often entails being relevant to the students' home cultures as well as
to their individual interests. It also entails enough variety of topic so
that the very different interests within a class can be met, and enough
variety of form so that students begin to deal with some of the
different sorts of material that are available, from newspaper comics
to posters recommending that they "Just say no" to cereal boxes to
songs to stories. Second, the materials need to be readable. "Readable" does not mean meeting some sort of readability formula; on
the contrary, materials written to such formulas are almost always
less readable than "real" stories, poems, articles, and letters (Goodman
et al. 1988; Rigg 1986). "Readable" means that students must be
able to build meaning from the print. That, in turn, means students
must be able to predict the overall structure of the piece and must
be able, as they progress through a piece, to predict with increasing
confidence. For example, if students read "Once upon a time," they
need to know without being told that they will be reading a narrative
in which a character tries to accomplish something and meets different
obstacles along the way. If they read "The first step in assembling . . ."
they need to know without being told that they will be reading a set
of directions, and that step one needs to be completed before
attempting step two, and so on. Not only the structure needs to be
predictable; so does some of the language. The phrase "Run, run,
as fast as you can; you can't catch me: I'm the gingerbread man!" is
repeated four or five times in the popular children's story, and before
the story is over, the students are not only predicting that the
gingerbread man will challenge the next character he meets, they
are also sure of the exact language of that challenge.

Beginning literacy is basically the same as advanced literacy; they
are not separate processes demanding different materials and teaching
techniques (Harste, Woodward, and Burke 1984). Any attempt to
break language into isolated words or letters destroys language and

makes literacy processes harder, not easier, to learn. LEA uses the whole language, not pieces, and uses students' strengths in the new language. The vocabulary is theirs; the grammatical structures are theirs; the overall structure of the piece is theirs; and most important, the topics are theirs, coming from their backgrounds and their interests. LEA uses the students' ideas phrased their way, which produces material that is highly predictable to those students. And the more predictable, the easier it is to read.

## Application

*Technique—Discussing*

An LEA session starts with a clear purpose and a clear audience. These determine, to a large extent, both content and form. The students will need time to discuss what they want to say, and the teacher can best serve as a discussion leader, one who listens much more than talks, and who speaks only when the discussion is veering far off the topic or on those rare occasions when a dispute needs to be settled by arbitration. The discussion often takes a great deal of time. It should be allotted plenty, since it is in the discussion that the students try out both their ideas of what should be dictated and the forms in which these ideas will be phrased. Also, if there is not adequate discussion, the dictated text will likely be rambling to the point of incoherency, particularly among the early grades.

What sorts of topics are appropriate? Whatever interests those particular students. Do they like to cook and eat, preparing, perhaps, peanut butter candy, or, inspired by the story, would they enjoy cooking a pot of stone soup? Those recipes can be LEA materials, dictated by the students as they prepare to cook. Are they interested in themselves, as most of us are? Each student can be Very Important Person of the Day, interviewed by a couple of classmates the previous day, and the VIP and classmates together prepare an oral report to the class, and a short biographical statement to dictate. Do they have pets? Funny stories about a pet are standard in elementary school, but to these can be added information about the care and feeding of this sort of animal. All of the topics that interest any student of this age are possibilities—family, crafts, etc. Perhaps some want to retell the story they've just heard the teacher read to them, so that they have a copy they themselves can read. Perhaps a group of students wants to use the pattern from a piece of children's literature, but put their own words to the pattern. The big book *Mrs. Wishy-*

*Washy* (Wright Group) was a favorite among some kindergartners and first graders I knew; they used the simple, repeated lines ("Oh, lovely mud," said the _____. And the _____ jumped into the mud.) as a pattern, replacing the pig, cow, and goose of the text with horse, dog, and cat, and illustrating the new book themselves. Bill Martin, Jr.'s *Brown Bear, Brown Bear* offered the pattern to another group of kindergartners; they used the repeated line, "_____ _____, what do you see? I see a _____ _____ looking at me," and substituted their own names and drawings of themselves. This particular book was the first the class had made this way, and since they made it the first week of school, not only were they all reading right off, they were learning each others' names and how to write them.

For the REAL students, there is a special topic: What are the newcomers' reactions to the United States of America and the U.S. school system? Telling someone how it feels to be the new one, the one who doesn't speak the language, and having that written down for everyone to read can be a giant step towards better understanding in the class. Another favorite is, "What would you tell a kid who will be in this class next year?"

The students who are creating the LEA material must have their own purposes for dictating, for wanting someone to write down these particular ideas. They must also have real people in mind to whom they want to read what they have dictated. Both authenticity of audience and variety of audience are important. Who will receive the final written product? Often the students themselves are the audience, as when the whole class wants a copy of their version of *The Gingerbread Man*, or when everyone wants to read a song they've just learned to sing. Other audiences are other students, as in a pen pal situation, or students across the hall or in another building. For example, secondary students could prepare big books of folktales for youngsters in K–2, using LEA, with the native speakers of English acting as scribes for the ESL students, who dictate stories from their countries and cultures.

I do not mean to imply that the teacher does all of the writing for the students. I am assuming that the students are also writing daily, again for their own purposes and to audiences of their own choosing. Dictation to the teacher produces material that all members of the dictating group can read, whereas often only the beginning writer can read what she or he has written. The principles underlying LEA are the same ones on which current writing instruction is based (Graves 1983; Calkins 1986; Atwell 1987). The primary principle is authenticity of task, as Edelsky (1986) points out. A second principle is that writing is not, except in graveyards, written in stone; there must be ample opportunity to try different ideas and different expressions of those ideas. In writing, these explorations are carried out through various drafts; in LEA the students explore their options through discussion. A third principle of writing instruction that is based on recent research is the role of editing: only when a writer decides to publish does editing become important. Until then, the focus is on expressing ideas with grace and vigor, not on conventional forms of spelling, punctuation, or grammatical structures.

## Technique—Dictating

After the all-important discussion, students tell their scribe what they want to say. Not all students want to dictate. Most teachers know that student participation is not only a matter of the student talking, and do not demand that each student dictate something. The scribe is usually the teacher, but certainly can be a teacher's aide, a community member, or another student acting as peer tutor. The scribe needs to write legibly on blackboard, overhead, or newsprint, at least legibly enough for the group to read what they've dictated. It's a good idea to leave plenty of space, so that revision is relatively easy. The students need to see their dictations being written, and the scribe needs to repeat what is being written at the same time. Students who have access to word processors are especially fortunate; they can work in pairs, dictating and typing into the computer the piece they are composing together. Revision is so easy it's almost fun, and many computers have programs to assist the editing step.

Tutors need to sit parallel with the students and write so that the students can see their words being written down, and not try to read them upside down or through the tutor's arm. After each sentence or phrase, the scribe rereads aloud, running a finger quickly under the lines. The scribe should not point at each word, much less read

> one
> word
> at
> a
> time.

That makes a word list; and word lists are not nearly as readable as connected text. As a matter of fact, I'd like to discourage any focus on individual words at all. Fragmenting the language makes it harder to read.

The scribe needs to reread each sentence more than once: repetition helps the students remember what they have said, and memorization of the text without any conscious effort to do so helps the beginning readers later read the text they have dictated. The scribe probably needs to indicate that one purpose for this rereading is to allow the students many opportunities to revise; another is to check on whether the scribe has accurately heard what the students dictated. I constantly ask, "Did I write what you wanted?" "Do you want me to change anything?"

### Technique—Accepting without Correcting

It is vital that the teacher or tutor accept the students' phrasing without correcting. If the students dictate an ungrammatical phrase, the scribe must write that ungrammatical phrase, and do it without any coy hints that it needs changing. The scribe cannot ask, "Are you sure that's the way you want it written? Does anyone here see any way to improve this sentence?" After writing the dictated phrase, the scribe reads it back as dictated, grammatical or not.

There are three major reasons for transcribing exactly what is dictated, without any discussion of grammar and without any "improvements" by the scribe. First, the primary purpose of LEA is to prepare reading material for the ESL students who are beginning to read in English. LEA material is readable because it is the students' ideas phrased the students' way; to change the phrasing makes the material less readable. Second, the LEA lesson should not be converted into a grammar lesson. Third, transcribing exactly what the students dictate gives information on what lessons the teacher should plan next and gives an excellent record of progress.

The first reason is the most important. LEA produces reading materials that the students can read and want to read, because LEA uses their ideas phrased their way. If it's the teacher's ideas or the teacher's phrasing, it is not LEA. LEA works because people can read what they have just said. It is more difficult to read what someone else has just said, but it is possible as long as what is said and the way that it is said correspond to one's own ideas and language forms. Sometimes a student will want to correct the phrasing of a classmate; when this happens I will make the suggested change only with permission from the author. This situation occurs infrequently, because the students contributing to a group LEA piece know that they will probably copy the final form of the piece, and will have several opportunities to make changes in their own copies.

The second reason for writing exactly what is dictated is that the focus should be on the piece itself, the material the students are learning to read even as they dictate it. I don't want to destroy the reading by focusing attention on tiny fragments of language, such as adding articles or changing verb forms. Of course my students dictate things like "old woman and old man and little boy," but if I stop their discussion and dictation to point out that I want an *a* before *little boy,* and an *an* before *old,* I've ruined everything. I've stopped both the dictating and the reading. I've made it clear that I consider standard adult grammatical forms much more important than my students' ideas.

Some people object to writing exactly what the students say, because they believe that this reinforces bad habits and that the students will never learn good English if they see incorrect English written by their teacher. I don't think so. The teacher records and repeats the students' sentences. That may be reinforcing to some students sometimes, but what is being reinforced—the idea, the form in which the idea is stated, the social involvement, all of these? All of the research done on both first- and second-language acquisition makes it clear that language is not a set of habits learned through stimulus-response conditioning, as behaviorists thought forty years ago. It has been clear for many years now that we develop language by trying things, by taking risks, and this, of course, often results in errors. Errors now are viewed as indicators of growth in language, not as symptoms of diseased language to be stamped out.

The scribe needs to use conventional spelling at all times, and not attempt to reproduce the students' pronunciation. You say *tomah-to,* I say *tomay-to,* but we both spell it *tomato.*

The third reason for writing exactly what the students dictate is to record examples of their present usage, examples that can suggest to the teacher what sort of instruction is needed next. This sort of information is invaluable to the teacher who is individualizing the class, and to the one who wants to individualize but doesn't know quite where to begin. The old axiom "Begin where the student is" is splendid advice, but first one needs to find out where the student is. Recording what each student says as each student says it helps to find out. Also, the LEA pieces provide a running record of progress in the language, a record the student and teacher both can refer to. A student who dictates "One from they . . ." and later that month, when rereading the dictation, self-corrects to "One of them . . ." (Rigg 1981) is indicating increasing control over English pronoun forms and English prepositions.

Sometimes a student will ask about the form. "What's the word for _____?" "How do you say _____?" "Should I say _____ or should I say _____?" When a student asks a question like this, I think someone should answer, the teacher or a classmate. There is a difference between not correcting the students' language and not addressing the students' questions: I believe in addressing their questions, and in encouraging students to collaborate in addressing those questions.

*Technique—Revising*

The students are most likely to ask such questions after the material has been dictated and they are rereading it and considering how to improve it. They may suggest changes of both their own and their classmates' contributions. I think the author is the only one who can make alterations, so if someone suggests changing a classmate's contribution, I always ask the classmate's permission. Students need practice in revising, and their initial attempts should be encouraged, so that the idea of revision as a natural part of composition will be nurtured. The sorts of revisions that I have seen most frequently involve changing sentences and moving sentences. The kinds of changes within sentences range from reordering within the sentence, and perhaps inserting or omitting something, to some minute feature that is more editing than revision, such as an -s or -ed on the end of a word. The following example of revision shows the movement of sections within the piece, similar to cut-and-staple in writing drafts, as well as omission of repetitious phrases.

First dictation by a group of six:

> She is a mother. Baby sick. Mother tired. Baby tired and sick. Mother hold baby. Picture on wall. This picture is different. The mother, baby very happy. Mother rest to the wall. She hair black.

Revision immediately after dictation:

> She is a mother with her baby. She has black hair. Baby is tired. The mother too, because the baby is sick. She is resting to the wall. There is a picture on the wall. This picture is different, because the mother, baby very happy.

*Technique—Follow-up*

After the group is satisfied with the material, students may want a copy. As with any written material, the purposes and uses determine whether it should be kept, and if so, in what form—individual typed copy, individual copy handwritten by the student, large copy on newsprint, large copy on board, copy on acetate for overhead. If the initial copy is on acetate for the overhead or on newsprint, the teacher or aide can type a copy and make duplicates. Some sorts of material require a large, clear master copy prominently displayed in the classroom, so that it can be referred to easily and frequently. One example is a daily calendar, with dictated material about the weather, about important events of the day (a birthday, a holiday), and about the Very Important Person of the Day. Some charts need to be kept, especially those of students' opinions, such as hypotheses (What do you think will happen to _____, and why?) or preferences (Which is the best way to _____ and why?). Recipes the students use need to be posted (stone soup: find one gray rock; get a big pot, etc.).

The students learn to read this material through rereading. As with the creation of the material, the rereading needs to be authentically motivated. Most students enjoy reading and rereading their LEA stories, whether they are retellings of folktales that the teacher has read to them or are original narratives that the students themselves have created. If the LEA material is a recipe, it will be reread if the students cook that particular dish again. If the material is a chart of class hypotheses, it will be reread as the hypotheses are tested. If the material is a brief biography of the day's Very Important Person, that VIP student will reread the material several times during the day, as will a few of the VIP's friends. If, on the other hand, the students have no real reason to reread the LEA material, there's little point in keeping a copy.

One way to use individual copies of the LEA material is as a starter for the students' own writing. "Here's what we created in our group yesterday; see what sorts of changes you want to make, and add on anything you feel like," the teacher says, and lets the students take individual ownership of their group product. Very young students often enjoy illustrating the material.

Often students and parents are concerned with individual words: they want to know which words can be "recognized." A teacher can try to educate both student and parent to understand that, first, reading is not a matter of recognizing words; second, recognizing words out of context is much harder than reading them in context; and last, that substituting one synonymous word for another when reading is a mark of a proficient reader. Meanwhile, the teacher who feels this sort of pressure can give each student an individual copy and ask them to draw a line under everything they can read. This focuses on the positive and on the students recognizing their own ability. Some teachers encourage the students to copy each word onto a 3" × 5" card, and to keep these cards as a sort of "word bank." Some students like such an activity and use their collection as a kind of private dictionary.

## Potential Problems

The most serious problem with having students dictate some of their initial reading material is that the students themselves may not write. They (and even the teacher) may view writing as somehow beyond them, because the teacher is writing for them. To prevent this problem, the students should spend much more time writing than they do dictating LEA material to the teacher. Again, they need authenticity of audience and of purpose (Edelsky 1986): they need to be composing stories, reports, invitations, and journals, real ones, not pretend ones done for teacher evaluation. Much of what a student writes will be readable only by that student for some months, but that is all right. An individual's beginning writing can sometimes be the basis for some LEA work, which often has a broader audience (i.e., more people can read it than a single author).

A second potential problem is caused when too many students are in the group producing the LEA material. Four to eight students make a nice sized group; more than that can easily result in too many voices at once, too little participation by some, and even disinterest or boredom on the part of some. If a class is already organized so that the students are engaged in a variety of tasks, working individually, in pairs, and in small groups, then it's easy to hold the LEA session as one of several group activities. Teachers who have not organized their classes this way, and who prefer always to have all of their students do the same activities at the same time, will probably not care much for the LEA process.

Teachers who have not used LEA before worry about moving from LEA material into commercially published material. Actually, students who are just beginning to read in English need a chance to look at commercially published literature from the start. With youngsters in grades K–3, there are some excellent materials available from the Wright Group, Rigby Publishers, and Scholastic. All three of these publishing companies offer big books, giant-sized versions of children's literature, which allow all of the students to see the illustrations as the teacher reads the material aloud to them. Rhodes's (1981) bibliography of predictable books for these grades and Atwell's

(1985) bibliography of predictable books for secondary students present two lists of literature that work well with beginning readers of different ages.

It's often a good idea, before reading any material, for the students to participate in a discussion about that material, just as before dictating an LEA piece, the students discuss what they want in it, how they want it structured, and how they want the sentences phrased. Creating a semantic web of predictions can make the actual reading of the material much easier. This is a sort of variation of LEA: it uses the students' ideas about what they are going to read and fosters their thinking about and discussing what they are likely to find. This makes the material more readable.

## Language Experience Approach—Reading Naturally

It's tempting to write a slogan and coin an acronym (LEARN, for example) for the language experience approach, tempting to "sell" it, because it is an enjoyable, natural, relatively easy way to get reading material for the new reader of English. Students dictating their ideas in their own phrasing see that their ideas and their phrases are so important to the teacher and the class that they are written down, just as presented, for everyone to see. Of course those students can read what they have just dictated; perhaps much more important is the recognition and respect they receive. I don't know of any other reading material that does that.

## References

Atwell, M. 1985. Predictable Books for Adolescent Readers. *Journal of Reading*, October: 18–22.

Atwell, N. 1987. *In the Middle: Writing, Reading and Learning with Adolescents*. Upper Montclair, N.J.: Boynton/Cook.

Calkins, L. M. 1986. *The Art of Teaching Writing*. Portsmouth, N.H.: Heinemann.

Edelsky, C. 1986. *Writing in a Bilingual Program: Había una Vez*. Norwood, N.J.: Ablex.

Goodman, K. S., Y. Freeman, S. Murphy, and P. Shannon. 1988. *Report Card on Basal Readers*. New York: Richard C. Owen.

Graves, D. 1983. *Writing: Teachers and Children at Work*. Portsmouth, N.H.: Heinemann.

Harste, J. C., V. A. Woodward, and C. L. Burke. 1984. *Language Stories and Literacy Lessons*. Portsmouth, N.H.: Heinemann.

Rhodes, L. 1981. I Can Read! Predictable Books as Resources for Reading and Writing Instruction. *Reading Teacher* 34:511–18.

Rigg, P. 1981. Beginning to Read in English the LEA Way. In *Reading English as a Second Language, Moving from Theory: Monograph 4 in Language and Reading*, edited by C. Twyford, W. Diehl, and K. Feathers, 81–90. Bloomington: Indiana University, School of Education.

———. 1986. Reading in ESL: Learning from Kids. In *Children and ESL: Integrating Perspectives*, edited by P. Rigg and D. S. Enright. Washington, D.C.: TESOL.

# 6 Encouraging and Understanding the Visual and Written Works of Second-language Children

Elizabeth A. Franklin
University of North Dakota, Grand Forks

Often, when working with second-language children, we focus heavily on how different these children are from the native-English-speaking children in our classrooms. Our perceptions of difference limit both what we allow the second-language children to show us and what we ultimately are able to learn about the children themselves. If we erroneously believe that they cannot express themselves appropriately using oral or written English, we may not offer opportunities for them to explore and express their ideas, interests, and preferences (Brown 1979; Flores 1982; Franklin 1984, 1985; Long and Sato 1983; Nystrom 1983; Pica and Long 1986; Ramirez and Stromquist 1979; Schinke-Llano 1983). Exercises on isolated literacy skills such as pattern drills, yes-no questions, flashcards, and worksheets do not encourage self-expression. Nor do such exercises enable teachers to know their students in any significant way. Time spent on drills and worksheets is time lost to both student and teacher.

Classrooms should be places where each child's individuality is recognized and valued, and this holds for the students speaking English as another language as well as for those who speak English as their only language. It is too easy to believe that language and cultural differences prevent second-language children from expressing who they are and prevent teachers from knowing these children and teaching to their strengths. Recent research involving the reading and writing processes of second-language children has demonstrated that ESL children do, indeed, explore and express meaning when they read and write (Edelsky 1986; Franklin 1984; Goodman and Goodman 1978; Hudelson 1984, 1986; Rigg 1981; Urzúa 1987). This chapter uses one child's drawings and compositions as an example of such exploration and expression, and an example of how much a teacher can learn from studying the child's creations.

For several summers, I taught reading and language to kindergarten and first grade Hispanic migrant children. A portion of every day was set aside for the children to produce creative written and visual works. The children frequently wrote or drew their responses to the stories that I had read aloud to them in class. They also wrote original poems and stories, created original visual works using pencils, crayons, markers, yarn, pâpier-mâché, and paints, and they dictated language experience stories to accompany some of their art work. These activities permitted the children to express themselves; moreover, my study of their creative works helped me to know my students more significantly.

The premise that teachers can know their students from the creative works they produce has been explored by King (1987) and Carini (1979). King argues that the aesthetic mode is the primary mode of cognition. Children express who they are and what they know in their gesture and tone, in their constructions and their play, and in their compositions and visual works. Therefore, children's works can be studied as serious aesthetic objects in the same way that one can study a painting by Picasso or a short story by Hemingway. What an artist chooses to paint tells us something about the artist; how that artist paints what was selected tells us even more. In order to study aesthetic preferences and meanings expressed by the children in my classroom, I used a procedure called "reflective observation," developed by Patricia Carini (1979). Through the careful study and description of the themes, genre, subject matter, characterization, color, line, composition, and style of language found in the children's works, I learned about the children themselves. In this chapter, I will discuss the creative written and visual works produced by a child whom I will call Maria. I worked with Maria during two summer school sessions. Of the many works that she produced, I am able to describe only nineteen: nine of these are visuals—seven drawings, one watercolor, one yarn drawing. The written compositions include one original story, two responses to stories read aloud in class, and several language experience stories. The themes and characters in her written works, the subject matter, composition, line, and color of her artworks, and the stylistic techniques and conventions found in her writing and art will be described in order to show how Maria herself shines through her works. Reflecting on her works helped me to know, value, and respect Maria.

## Creating Visual Works

Two art activities occurred on a regular basis in my classroom. Children responded artistically to the stories read aloud to them in class by making drawings or paintings of their favorite character or episode in a story. Children also were given many opportunities to draw or paint anything they wished.

### Artistic Responses to Literature

In kindergarten, the children listened to many fairy and folktales in both Spanish and English, including *Cinderella, Goldilocks and the Three Bears, The Three Billy Goats Gruff, Sleeping Beauty, The Little Red Hen*, and *Chicken Little*. After listening to a story, each child illustrated a favorite part or character. Their illustrations and any accompanying dictations were then made into books.

This type of art activity reveals a great deal about a child's interests and literary and aesthetic preferences. Children depict those characters or events in a story that they are drawn to for whatever reason. In addition, even if a group of children shares a common understanding of a story, each creates a different thematic interpretation. *The Gingerbread Boy*, for example, elicited very different interpretations. Some children focused on the adventures of the gingerbread boy and drew him running gleefully away from the old man and woman and all the animals he encountered. Other children focused on how delicious the gingerbread boy tasted to the fox, and they drew the fox licking his lips and grinning. There were always a few children who focused on the loss the old man and woman felt when the boy ran away; they drew the old man and woman crying, and one child drew a funeral in a cemetery. Studying the children's illustrations can give teachers a great deal of information about the variety of their students' interpretations.

Maria drew her favorite part of *Chicken Little*, the last episode in which Chicken Little learns that the sky is not really falling, and it was only a nut that hit her head. She also dictated that part of the story for me to write, so she could copy it onto her drawing. She remembered it so well that she dictated the exact text. (Here it is translated from the Spanish.)

> Oh, Chicken Little, the sky is not falling. What fell on your tail was this nut.

Maria chose to depict the resolution of the story, the happy ending, and did so very accurately. Her illustration and dictation were very closely tied together. It is interesting to note that she put a *100%* on the top of her page after she finished her work. These details demonstrate Maria's preference for accuracy and realism. She wanted to write and draw exactly what was in the original story. She also took great pains when writing to copy exactly. Other children in the group added new characters, changed the story line, or drew something totally unrelated to the original story.

Artistically, Maria's drawing and writing are orderly and balanced (Figure 1). She draws the five characters of the story, placing Chicken Little in the middle of the page with the other characters around her and looking at her. The five figures are equally spaced out along the bottom of the page. Each has a head, a beak, two eyes, wings, a body, and two legs with webbed feet. The written text fills in the space on the page not occupied by the drawing. In fact, Maria creates her own square picture on a rectangular piece of paper by separating her picture/text from her name (which has been deleted) and the number *100* at the top of the page. It is remarkable that Maria knew visually where to start writing her text so that the print would fill in her open space so completely and so neatly.

Figure 1

*Original Artwork*

When second-language children are given the opportunity to create their own original visual works, they express their interests, ideas, and preferences. Through studying the content and style of these works, a teacher can learn what is deeply important to the children.

When Maria was given the opportunity to draw anything she wished, she almost always drew a picture of her family or her home. Figure 2, a pencil drawing that Maria drew after kindergarten, shows her sister holding a balloon. The sister is centered on the page and drawn very large. The figure is also very solid, composed of geometric shapes. The legs are rectangular, as are the arms, neck, and torso. The face is round, with circles for eyes and half-circle shapes for eyebrows, mouth, and hair. Maria attempted to make the legs, arms, feet, and hands geometric and proportional to each other, as evidenced by her numerous erasures. The head was made larger, one arm was widened to match the other, one foot was turned the opposite direction, and the left line of the torso was straightened out. All of these changes were made to maintain balance and ensure sameness and proportion of body parts. In addition, Maria erased the *A* balloon and made a *B* balloon, possibly to stand for the word *balloon*, which she subsequently realized was in her dictated text. She also moved the balloon from the left to the right side of the picture, and by doing so created a more balanced effect.

Figure 3 is a crayon drawing, also made after kindergarten, of a large house with eight windows, five flowers growing outside, and a sun shining in the sky. The house, consisting of squares, rectangles, and triangles, creates a strong sense of geometric design. It is also very large and solid, as are the windows. The largeness and openness of the windows create an inviting effect in much the same way as the smile of her sister in Figure 2. Maria's preference for symmetrical order dominates the drawing. Although the door of the house is placed asymmetrically, the windows and flowers are all symmetrically arranged and three smaller windows are systematically set around a large window in the attic. The two windows of the house itself are placed in the uppermost left- and right-hand corners. There are also two windows in the front door, each equidistant from the doorknob and one positioned directly on top of the other. The five large flowers, made almost exactly alike, are lined up neatly on both sides of the house, filling up the space between the house and the edges of the paper.

Although color and type of strokes cannot be perceived in the reproductions here, Maria uses light, soft strokes with her crayons,

I love
my    sister.
Her   name
is
She   has
one   balloon.

Figure 2

primarily all in the same direction. She colored the house red, the roof blue, and the flowers orange and green. Maria also outlined her house and most of the windows. She colored very carefully in order not to go beyond the lines that she had drawn. The lightness of her stroke and the softness in her colors, along with the openness expressed in the large windows, all contribute to a cheerful and warm tone. The sense of geometric design, the symmetry and balance, the large, solid, centered figures and objects, the cheerful and warm tone, and the methodical care with which she drew were evident in most of Maria's artwork. In both kindergarten and first grade, Maria made houses in essentially the same way (i.e., large, geometric, with windows in the corners). Her human figures were always large and block-like, yet smiling and cheerful.

Other children drew different kinds of subjects under these same circumstances. Luis, for example, seemed fascinated by motion. In his action-filled pictures, he depicted exhaust coming out of a car, clouds moving across the sky, smoke billowing up from a chimney, and a small boy swinging on a swing set. His pictures were balanced aesthetically, but always asymmetrically. When he drew clouds, for example, Luis made no effort to make them all alike or to line them up evenly in the sky. Another child, Rosa, drew pictures of people doing things. When she drew herself, she was reading in school or playing baseball. When she drew her family, they were driving to

Figure 3

Mexico in their truck. Her pictures were rapidly drawn, with little attention paid to the outline. Rosa preferred color to line. Her pictures were frequently solidly and brightly colored.

Detailed observation of these children's artworks provided me with important insights about each child's interests and aesthetic preferences. Maria prefers the clarity of geometric forms, the solidity of large, symmetrical objects, and the softness of light strokes and colors. Luis prefers a more fluid design, spiraling and round asymmetrical shapes, and the energy that emanates from motion. Rosa, on the other hand, likes action, but the action that comes from people doing things individually (such as reading or playing ball) or in groups (such as traveling to Mexico). Rosa uses rapid strokes, drawing the outline of her objects without a great deal of concern. Her coloring is done with strong strokes and brilliant hues.

All children express something of their interests and preferences in their creative visual works. Teachers who allow children to create visual works have an opportunity to know their children in personal and significant ways. When differences among children are observed, valued, and respected, classrooms become better learning environments. As Maria's teacher, I began to observe how the aesthetic preferences evident in her art influenced her work in other subject areas. With Luis, who was a very quiet child, I gained insights about his interests in motors and mechanized movement and planned some reading activities around these interests. With Rosa, who was very difficult to handle in class because she was constantly active and constantly talking with the other children, I learned to respect her strengths. Through studying her visual works, I was able to focus on her positive and valuable aspects and to place her classroom behavior within a larger framework.

## Creating Written Work

Several kinds of writing activities occurred regularly in my classroom, and these resulted in the children producing creative written works. The children dictated or wrote their own texts to accompany their artworks; they wrote responses to literature that was read aloud in class; and they wrote original stories.

### Texts Accompanying Pictures

Maria's writing displays many of the same characteristics as her art. This is the text which Maria dictated to accompany the drawing of her sister (Figure 2):

> I love my sister. Her name is ______. She has one balloon.

The text that Maria dictated to accompany her house drawing (Figure 3) was in Spanish. The English translation is:

> I love my mother. I love my father.

By first grade, Maria did all of her own writing, no longer dictating language experience materials to the teacher. Figure 4 is a text that she wrote to accompany a picture of a house, flowers, trees, and birds, drawn in first grade. It reads:

> I love my mother and my father. I love my sisters and my brothers. I love my pet. And my dolls. And my uncle J.R.

All three texts speak of Maria's love for her real family. She details in her accumulated work the real people and real things that she cares about. Other children, given the opportunity to write or dictate anything they wish, describe objects such as cars or bikes, rather than people, or they may invent humorous stories. Maria focuses on her feelings in her writings: all three compositions start with "I love," and she repeats this, listing the family members whom she loves.

Stylistically, the sense of symmetry and balance that was evident in her visual work also appears in her written work. The same sentence patterns are repeated throughout. In the dictation about her mother and father, both sentences follow the pattern *SVO* (Subject Verb Object). In the longer text (Figure 4) she uses SVO, but makes the object a compound one, and she systematically repeats this. Perhaps the reason for Maria's systematic pattern is that English is her second language, and she is only beginning to read and write: perhaps she's found one pattern she controls and sticks to it. Other children who are learning ESL and becoming literate do not use the same exact patterns, however, as Maria does. Also, a whole year had passed between the time Maria dictated the two sentences about loving her mother and father and the time she wrote the five sentences

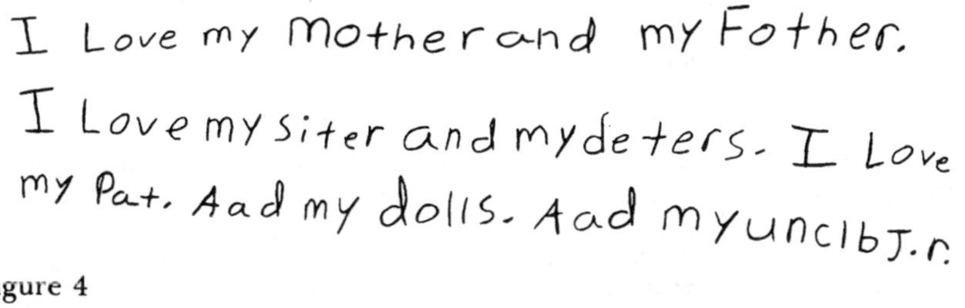
I Love my Motherand myFother.
I Love mysiter and mydeters. I Love
my Pat. Aad my dolls. Aad myunclbJ.r.

Figure 4

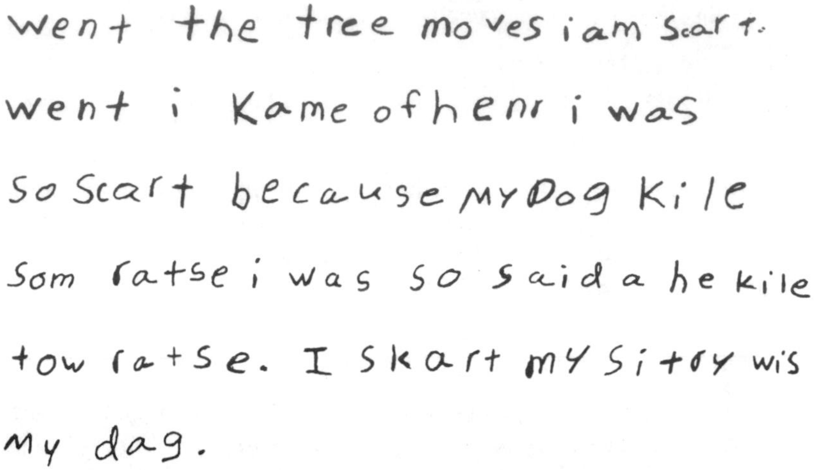

went the tree moves i am scart.
went i Kame ofhenr i was
so scart because MyDog Kile
Som ratse i was so said a he kile
tow ratse. I skart mY sitry wis
My dag.

Figure 5

about loving her family. Although Maria had become a much more fluent user of English, she still preferred certain subjects and certain stylistic uses.

*Written Responses to Literature*

Children's literature serves many important functions in the classroom. As they explore the themes in books, children learn more about their own ideas and interests (Yolen 1981). Two children's books that Maria liked and responded to in writing were *It Didn't Frighten Me* (Goss and Harste 1981) and *The Magic Fish* (Littledale 1966). Both are picture books, which helps an ESL child to pick up the sense of the story from the pictures. Also, both books use a repetitive sentence which ESL students quickly learn to understand.

After listening to *It Didn't Frighten Me*, the class was asked to write about something that frightens them. Maria wrote (Figure 5):

> When the tree moves I am scared. When I came over here I
> was so scared because my dog killed some rats. I was so sad and
> he killed two rats. I scared my sister with my dog.

After listening to *The Magic Fish*, the children were asked to write what they would wish for if they caught a magic fish. Maria wrote (Figure 6):

> If I had a wish I will be happy. I could have some dolls. I could
> have so many dolls for a castle. And I could have a magic fish.

> And I could have so many fishes. I would have so many money.
> I wish so many flowers. I want a cheese. I wish I had a party.

In her response to *It Didn't Frighten Me,* Maria describes three different incidents that frighten her. The first incident ("When the tree moves I'm scared.") is tied to the story and reflects Maria's empathy with the main character, who imagines all kinds of things in the tree outside his window at night. Then she describes two real-life incidents, both involving her dog. The assignment encourages the expression of emotion; Maria uses *so* twice to express the intensity of her feelings ("I was so scared . . . I was so sad"). Maria's aesthetic preferences and interests are evident in this composition. In contrast to some of the children, who wrote about supernatural or imaginary events, Maria focused on real-life situations in which she had been involved, and on her personal reactions to these incidents. Other children described incidents they had heard about from a relative, rather than incidents in which they were present. Maria reported three incidents, whereas most of the children reported only one. This demonstrates her preference for accuracy: when asked to describe something that frightened her, she wanted to be as complete and thorough as possible.

Ifi had awich i will be happy.
I could have Some dolls.
I could have so mohe dolls for
a kasle. Aad I could have a
migic fihe. Aad i could have
so mobe fihes. fihe i wobe have
so mohe mone. I wehe so mohe florws
I went a sches. I wehe i hadte
a Pray.

Figure 6

Some of these same preferences show up in Maria's response to *The Magic Fish*. Again she is not content to describe only one wish, as many children did; instead, she thinks of every possible thing she might wish for. Although she does wish for a magical fish, all of her other wishes are for real, everyday things like dolls, money, flowers, cheese, and a party. Maria continues to be the center of her composition: in every sentence, the pronoun *I* is the subject. It is used eleven times. Maria again uses *so* as an intensifier; she uses "so many" and "so much" four times. And again she writes about her feelings, her responses to the events and people in her life.

*Original Stories and Poems*

The last type of activity I want to discuss is the writing of original stories and poems. When children write their own stories and poems, they express their ideas, interests, and aesthetic preferences in the themes they develop, the characters they invent, the images they describe, and the language they utilize.

In first grade Maria wrote an original story about a bear (Figure 7). It reads:

> The bear likes to eat honey. The bear will have a party tomorrow. The bear will have so much fun. The bear will have so much friends. The bear will eat so much honey. The bear will play in the sun with his friends.

This is a story about friendship. Maria describes a bear who is having a party, who has friends, and who plays with those friends. When she

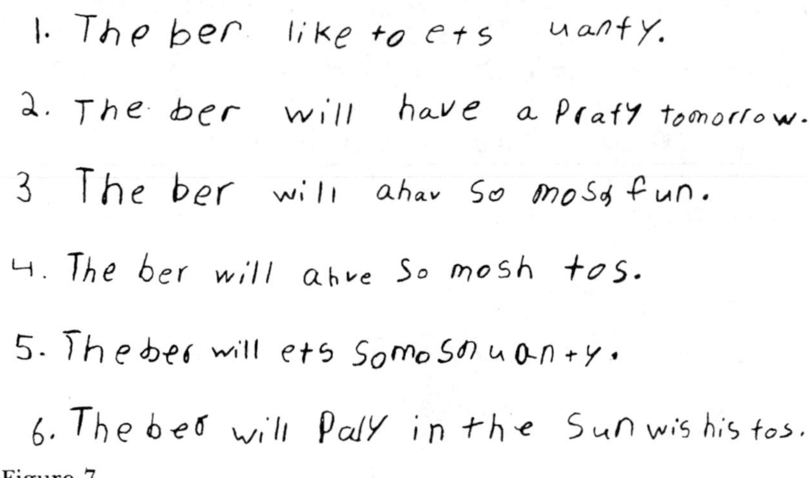

1. The ber like to ets uanty.

2. The ber will have a Prafy tomorrow.

3 The ber will ahav So mosd fun.

4. The ber will ahve So mosh tos.

5. The ber will ets Somosn uanty.

6. The ber will Paly in the Sun wis his tos.

Figure 7

drew and wrote her responses to literature, Maria demonstrated a preference for subjects related to her family and home. In this fictional writing, she seems to transform this preference into a theme of friendship and human relationships.

Maria's preference for symmetry shows again in her story of the bear. All of the sentences begin "the bear" and five of the six sentences use the auxiliary "will" plus verb, followed by an object or by prepositional phrases. She uses "so much" three times, again intensifying her statements. Also, Maria numbers her sentences. This may be a personal convention which helps her focus on the quantity of ideas and on their order; however, because this story was written during the first week of summer school, it is also possible that Maria is carrying a convention of basal exercises over into her creative writing.

The writing of poetry nurtures expression in second-language as well as first-language children. Figure 8 contains three of the eight poems that Maria wrote after hearing "The Magical Mouse" (by Kenneth Patchen, see Gensler and Myhart 1978). The children were all asked to write and illustrate their own poems, using Patchen's as a model. To ease the children into their first experiences writing poetry, a visiting poet suggested that they start their poems with the phrase "I am the magical _____" and then follow this line with descriptive statements about the qualities that their magical animal possessed. The children were also shown how to write descriptive statements beginning with "I do," "I don't," "I like," and "I don't like." Maria wrote:

> I am the magical rabbit.
> I don't jump.
> I don't sleep.
>
> I am the magical dog.
> I do fly.
> I do ride a bike.
>
> I am the magical mouse.
> I do like cheese.
> I do like to play with other mice.
> I do like to run fast.

Maria wrote poems about a magical rabbit, dog, cat, mouse, frog, bird, lamp, and apple. Seven poems had three lines each and one poem had four lines. Maria explored different line patterns across the different poems. For example, in the rabbit poem, she used the pattern "I don't" plus verb; in the dog poem, she used "I do" plus verb. In none of the eight poems did she mix the patterns. In fact,

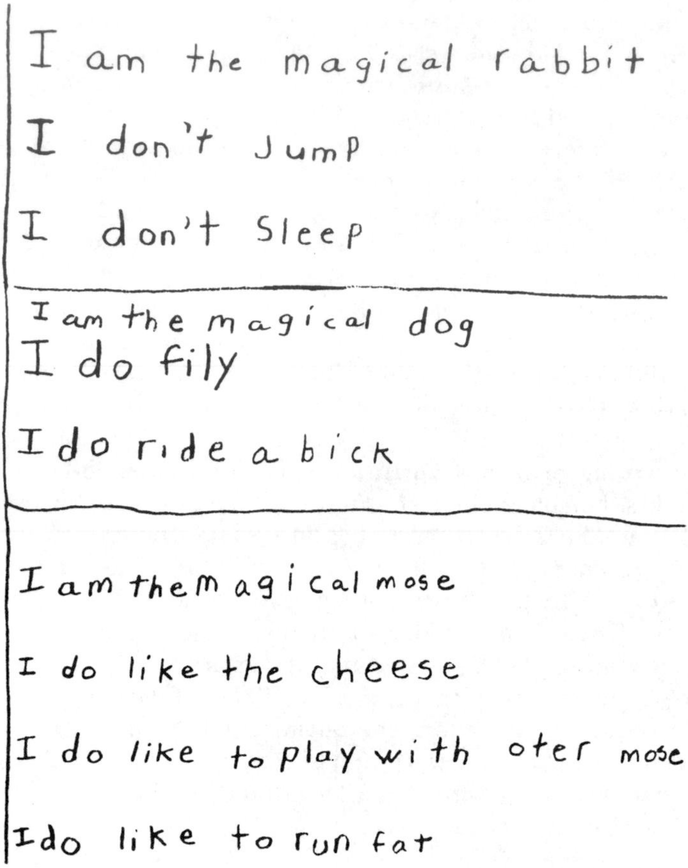

I am the magical rabbit

I don't Jump

I don't Sleep

---

I am the magical dog
I do fily

I do ride a bick

---

I am the magical mose

I do like the cheese

I do like to play with oter mose

I do like to run fat

Figure 8

when looking at the order in which she wrote the poems, one sees that Maria systematically alternates her use of *do* and *don't*. She also drew lines to separate one poem from another.

Other children in the class explored different techniques. Most wrote only two poems, but each poem had five or six lines. In addition, other children used *do* and *don't* lines in the same poem. Maria's aesthetic preference for symmetry and balance guided her poetry as it guided her art and other compositions.

Maria also systematically explored different kinds of images in her poems. In two of the eight poems, she was able to create a magical animal by taking a couple of common qualities of the animal and negating them. Her magical rabbit, for example, does not jump or sleep. In four of her poems about magical animals, she went further, creating fantastic images. Her magical dog, for example, flies and rides a bike; her magical lamp doesn't run or work; her magical apple plays and flies; and her magical cat doesn't like computers and doesn't laugh. What most impresses me, though, are Maria's two poems with realistic qualities of the animals: her mouse likes cheese, other mice, and running fast; her bird likes to fly and sing. Just as in her kindergarten year she had selected topics of family and home, so now she plays with magical qualities, but returns to the real and the well-known.

Maria varies the kinds of images she creates in her different poems. This variation, however, is as systematic and consistent within each individual poem as was the variation in type of line discussed previously. Maria does not mix the different types of images within one poem. Again, her desire for symmetry and an almost perfect balance influences choices she makes in her poems, choices which contrast with those made by other children in the class.

What did I learn about Maria from studying her art and writing? I learned that she liked to write about herself and important personal relationships; that she readily expressed her emotional reactions to events and people. Although she could create imaginary situations and characters, she preferred to write about and draw the things in her immediate, day-to-day existence. She demonstrated a preference for accuracy and completeness, wanting to depict stories, characters, and events as realistically and as thoroughly as possible. Finally, I learned that Maria preferred balance and symmetrical order, and that she achieved this through careful control of topic, sentence structure, and vocabulary in composition, and through careful placement of both drawing and text in her artwork.

## Learning about Art and Written Language

At the same time that Maria expressed her interests and aesthetic preferences in her creative works, she also demonstrated and explored her understanding of the forms, functions, and conventions of art and written language. Maria's works, discussed here, clearly show that she understands many of the stylistic and literary differences that occur among poetry, stories, and written responses to literature. The texts she produced were always appropriate for the context and the assignment, as were the artworks.

Maria's art and compositions also reveal her understanding and exploration of conventions in both art and writing. Although there is definitely a personal style evident in her work, the houses, flowers, trees, suns, and human figures that she draws reflect the conventional ways in which these objects are depicted in art by children in our society. With respect to writing conventions, Maria knows that she is supposed to capitalize the first word of a sentence and put a period at the end. Although her sentences are not always conventional, Maria always punctuates what she considers to be a sentence. Currently, Maria does not capitalize the pronoun *I* unless it begins a sentence. For this reason, although she initially capitalized the second *I* in Figure 5, she later erased it, and wrote a lower case *i*.

Maria's writing shows her learning a great deal about the conventions of the English orthographic system. She spelled both visually and phonetically. Her visual spellings are especially evident in words she has memorized (*like, could, laugh, happy*). Her phonetic spellings show her grappling with ways to represent words as they sounded to her (bear—*ber*, money—*mone*), and as they sound when she "sounds them out" (play—*paly*, fly—*fily*, rats—*ratse*). Maria had an extensive repertoire of graphic symbols to represent complex sounds. For example, she used the *y* to represent the long *i* in fly, and used *le* to represent the last syllable in castle—*kasle*. Although the end result is not a conventional spelling, it shows a great deal of intuitive language knowledge, as does the use of *ck* to represent the final *k* in bike, the use of *sh* for the final sound in much, and the use of *sk* for the initial sounds of scared. Maria also appears to be hypothesizing that some words end in silent *e*, because she added a final *e* to many of her words (fish—*fihe*, sing—*sime*). It is also possible that she was sounding out the words slowly and heard an extra vowel at the end.

ESL children learn a great deal about written language and art by participating in the creation of written and visual works. Maria, for example, quickly realized that writers do not number the sentences of their stories when she saw that the stories written by me and by the other children were not numbered. Thereafter, she did not number her sentences. She also learned how to express her ideas using different composition forms and different art materials. By actually writing and drawing to express herself, Maria learned a lot about writing and drawing (Harste, Woodward, and Burke 1984).

Although teachers can learn about a child's growing mastery over conventions of writing and of art, it is important not to focus primarily on these aspects. More important is the child's intent, the creative expression of that child's feelings and ideas. It is crucial to look first at the aesthetic dimensions of a child's work and value the work for its aesthetic qualities. If too much attention is paid to the developmental aspects of language learning or art learning, there is a danger of losing the child's individual voice and style. And if that happens, there is little reason for the child to read, write, draw, or paint.

## Helping Maria in the Classroom

Through studying Maria's art and compositions, I learned about her interests and aesthetic preferences. This knowledge helps me plan materials and activities for her. For example, since Maria prefers the subjects of human relationships and the emotions that are a part of those relationships, I look for books such as *Corduroy* (Freeman 1968), *Leo the Late Bloomer* (Kraus 1971), *Mr. Gumpy's Outing* (Burningham 1971), and Ormerod's wordless picture books *Moonlight* (1982) and *Sunshine* (1981). The illustrations, the predictable story line, and the resulting predictable text are highly appropriate for a second-language learner. I might try reading to Maria the long poem, *The Bear Who Saw the Spring* (Kuskin 1961), because it presents realistic and concrete images of the seasons. Maria needs to be offered art activities such as weaving, yarn and string art, and painting abstract designs, because these activities fit with her preference for symmetry and geometrical design. Also, science activities that involve systematic observation and recording of data fit Maria's preferences.

Carini's reflective observation offers teachers with ESL students a means of getting to know those students as individuals, to find out where they are. The first step is providing them with opportunities to express themselves in art and in composition; the second is learning from those works what kinds of ideas, interests, and preferences the ESL child has (as well as getting an idea of the child's English). The third step builds on the previous one: the teacher uses what he or she has learned about each child to provide learning experiences tailored to the individual. Throughout, the children see that their work is respected and valued, and they learn from this that they are, too.

## References

Brown, D. 1979. *Mother Tongue to English: The Young Child in the Multicultural School*. Cambridge: Cambridge University Press.

Burningham, J. 1971. *Mr. Gumpy's Outing*. New York: Holt, Rinehart and Winston.

Carini, P. 1979. *The Art of Seeing and the Visibility of the Person*. Grand Forks: North Dakota Study Group on Evaluation.

Edelsky, C. 1986. *Writing in a Bilingual Program: Había una Vez*. Norwood, N.J.: Ablex.

Flores, B. 1982. Language Interference or Influence: Toward a Theory for Hispanic Bilingualism. Unpublished doctoral dissertation, University of Arizona.

Franklin, E. 1984. A Naturalistic Study of Literacy in Bilingual Classrooms. Unpublished doctoral dissertation, Indiana University.

————. 1986. Literacy Instruction for LES Children. *Language Arts* 63: 51–60.

Freeman, D. 1968. *Corduroy*. New York: Scholastic.

Gensler, K., and N. Nyhart. 1978. *The Poetry Connection*. New York: Teachers and Writers.

Goodman, K., and Y. Goodman. 1978. *Reading of American Children Whose Language Is a Stable Rural Dialect of English or a Language Other than English*. Final Report, Project NIE-C-PD-3-0087. Washington, D.C.: Department of Health, Education, and Welfare.

Goss, J., and J. Harste. 1981. *It Didn't Frighten Me*. New York: School Book Fairs.

Harste, J., V. Woodward, and C. Burke. 1984. *Language Stories and Literacy Lessons*. Portsmouth, N.H.: Heinemann.

Hudelson, S. 1984. Kan Yu Ret an Rayt en Ingles: Children Become Literate in English as a Second Language. *TESOL Quarterly* 18:221–38.

————. 1986. ESL Children's Writing: What We've Learned, What We're Learning. In *Children and ESL: Integrating Perspectives*, edited by P. Rigg and D. S. Enright, 25–54. Washington, D.C.: TESOL.

King, R. 1987. The Primal Mode of Aesthetics in Children's Work and Play. *Insights* 20:1–15.

Kraus, R. 1971. *Leo the Late Bloomer*. New York: Windmill.

Kuskin, K. 1961. *The Bear Who Saw the Spring*. New York: Harper and Row.

Littledale, F. 1966. *The Magic Fish*. New York: Scholastic.

Long, M., and C. Sato. 1983. Classroom Foreigner Talk Discourse: Forms and Functions of Teachers' Questions. In *Classroom Oriented Research in Second Language Acquisition*, edited by H. Seliger and M. Long, 268–85. Rowley, Mass.: Newbury House.

Nystrom, N. J. 1983. Teacher-Student Interaction in Bilingual Classrooms: Four Approaches to Error Feedback. In *Classroom Oriented Research in Second Language Acquisition*, edited by H. Seliger and M. Long, 169–88. Rowley, Mass.: Newbury House.

Ormerod, J. 1981. *Sunshine*. New York: Puffin.

————. 1982. *Moonlight*. New York: Puffin.

Pica, T., and M. Long. 1986. The Linguistic and Conversational Performance of Experienced and Inexperienced Teachers. In *Talking to Learn: Conversation in Second Language Acquisition*, edited by R. Day, 85–98. Rowley, Mass.: Newbury House.

Ramirez, A., and N. Stromquist. 1979. ESL Methodology and Student Language Learning in Bilingual Elementary Schools. *TESOL Quarterly* 13:145–58.

Rigg, P. 1981. Beginning to Read in English the LEA Way. In *Reading English as a Second Language, Moving from Theory: Monograph 4 in Language and Reading*, edited by C. Twyford, W. Diehl, and K. Feathers, 81–90. Bloomington: Indiana University, School of Education.

———. 1986. Reading in ESL: Learning from Kids. In *Children and ESL: Integrating Perspectives*, edited by P. Rigg and D. S. Enright, 55–91. Washington, D.C.: TESOL.

Schinke-Llano, L. 1983. Foreigner Talk in Content Classrooms. In *Classroom Oriented Research in Second Language Acquisition*, edited by H. Seliger and M. Long, 268–85. Rowley, Mass.: Newbury House.

Urzúa, C. 1987. "You Stopped Too Soon": Second Language Children Composing and Revising. *TESOL Quarterly* 21:279–97.

Yolen, J. 1981. *Touch Magic*. New York: Philomel.

# 7 Putting Language Variation to Work for You

Carole Edelsky
Arizona State University, Tempe

Language varies. Over time. Across space. From situation to situation. This feature of language—its variability—is a boon to scholars (who can use language variation as indirect evidence of other social phenomena) and a blight to prescriptivists (who see variation as deviation from the One True Standard, a sign of deterioration). What is it to teachers who, like all people everywhere, participate with others (in the teachers' case, with their students) in varying situations and therefore varying language use? And what does it mean to teachers who not only experience language changing from situation to situation, but who additionally count among their mainstream, regional, standard-English-speaking students a few non-standard-English speakers and one or two who are just beginning to learn English? Is all that variety a problem to these teachers? Or is it a treasure?

What I hope to do in this chapter is present a particular perspective on one aspect of language variation (variation in students' native languages) and then offer some suggestions for how teachers can use another aspect of variation (variation according to situation) to turn a potential problem into a curricular asset. To do this, I will rely on a key sociolinguistic concept—communicative competence—and an important newly revived curricular area—writing.

## Language Varies "Internally"

No one talks or writes the same way in all situations to all audiences, and no two social groups use language in exactly the same way. In other words, language varies *within* a group of speakers (from situation to situation) and *between* groups of speakers (from dialect group to dialect group). But what exactly is it that varies? The answer to that question requires a very brief description of language.

Language is a socially shared system for making meaning. "System" means that subparts are interconnected and depend on each other; "making meaning" signifies that meaning is always socially created and, too, that every utterance is not only about what it refers to, but is also about the particular social situation (who is speaking, to whom, where, with what relation to that topic, etc.). The language Cagney and Lacey use about a case they are working on varies, for example, depending on whether they are talking about the case at their desks, in the lieutenant's office, or in the comparative privacy of the women's washroom. Language can be oral, written, or sign. Whatever its modality (sound, print, or hand gesture), language is made up of subsystems. If the language is oral, the subsystems are phonology (rules for categorizing and interpreting sounds), morphology (a subsystem for forming words and units of meaning like *plural*), syntax (a system for stringing words together to point out, state, negate, question, order, etc.), semantics (a set of rules for combining meanings), and pragmatics (a subsystem for creating and understanding utterances as tied to contexts). If the language is written or signed, instead of phonology the counterpart subsystems are graphics and orthography (written) and sign (including signs for units used in finger spellings).

To return now to the question of what it is exactly that varies when language is characterized as variable, the answer is: choices from each of these subsystems. There are different pronunciations depending on the setting and the addressee, different verb constructions depending on topic and genre, different ways to form a question depending on audience, different possible combinations of word meanings depending on purpose, different terms of address depending on the relationship between addressor and addressee.

These variations are not random; neither are the particular options within subsystems. People do not simply pronounce words, select verb tenses, or choose address terms, any old way no matter where they are or who is present. Two lovers wanting to express their affection do so differently if one of their mothers is in the room. Nor does language offer ways to encode anything and everything. Instead, what is available within subsystems embodies the group's history and concerns. And there are social norms for using certain options to construct certain meanings in certain contexts. The presence of choice within subsystems and the norms for choosing are what make it inevitable that people give off messages each time they give them (Goffman 1959). In other words, saying you're sorry by saying "oops" and apologizing by saying "please excuse my clumsiness" offers a message about who the speaker is, and what her relationship is to the "victim" as much as it expresses an apology.

Learning a language, then, as a baby learning her first or a seven-year-old or a twenty-seven-year-old learning his second, can never be a matter of learning one interpretation for any given language item. Depending on the context, that item can mean a variety of things. Someone learning a language has to learn just how that language item "depends" in what ways on just what features of that context. Being able to account for all this variation in producing and inter-preting choices within all the language subsystems in changing con-texts is what a native speaker of the language can do. Being able to deliberately use this variation in the service of language learning/ teaching is what a language educator must do. The formal term for this ability is "communicative competence" (Hymes 1970). One formal definition of communication competence is knowledge of the meanings of utterances, the meanings of situations, and the relation between the two (Hymes 1970).

Although in mainstream language arts education it is not usually expressed this way, the overriding goal of English-language educators is to enlarge the children's communicative competence in English. The aim is to help children expand their repertoires so that they can choose from a greater range within each subsystem, so they can learn through experience new occasions which call forth particular new choices, and so they can evoke some of those situations merely by making a particular language choice. This goal may seem difficult, however, for a teacher who has students with different language backgrounds. It becomes far easier if these teachers can intentionally put situational variation to work in the curriculum. But that requires an understanding of what "different language backgrounds" might mean.

## Language Varies "Externally"

People who agree on how to interpret variation in phonological, syntactic, semantic, and pragmatic choices; who share knowledge of utterances, situations, and the relation between the two; and who share norms for interpreting language depending on context belong to the same speech community. When people learn a second language, they are learning much more than a language; they are learning how to join a speech community.

Now it would seem that an older second-language learner would not need to learn about varying talk, depending on whom one is talking to, where one is, and so on. People who already know one language already know that. It is true; they do already know that variation exists, and they expect it in the second-language community, too, but they don't know how it works there. Norms for language use are specific to a given speech community. Not only do the choices of sounds, vocabulary, and syntax vary from speech community to speech community, but so do the ways of thinking about situations. Two speech communities may divide situations up differently to begin with, or they may define the "same" situation differently. For example, Navajo children delight in listening to stories about the coyote: an Anglo teacher may not have taken note of when coyote stories are told by the older Navajos, and may break a taboo by introducing such stories in class when it is not winter. The Navajo speech community carefully defines the time for telling coyote stories and other folktales; it must be between the first frost of winter and the first thunder of spring. The coyote stories can also serve as an example of the "same" situation being defined differently: to most teachers who do not know Navajo culture, these stories are similar to Grimm's animal folktales; to Navajos, these stories are much more than stories.

The range of possible human purposes for relating to others (and to oneself) is distributed and highlighted dissimilarly across the world's speech communities. For example, building rapport (with supporting purposes of getting close, showing interest, empathizing, etc.) might be a central motive in one group; avoiding imposition (with supporting purposes of permitting, accepting, etc.) could be the overarching orientation in another. (See Tannen 1984 for a study of two speech communities that contrast on these dimensions.) Brown and Levinson (1978) claim that underlying the surface variety there are two fundamental purposes which are universal: to be unimpeded in regard to one's desires, and at the same time, to be approved of. Whether considering these underlying universal purposes or those at a more surface level, it is clear that oral language, with its options within subsystems, is a major human resource for accomplishing one's purpose.

Written language is another. In most speech communities in North America, writing permits access to certain societal resources. As a tool for thinking, it offers new opportunities for reflecting, remembering, and reasoning. It permits interaction with people distant in space and time. It certainly enhances one's communicative competence, adding to one's repertoire of language-as-resource. Prodded by recent research in writing (Calkins 1983; Dyson 1982; Graves

1983), educators have begun to change their schedules as well as their thinking about literacy in order to give writing a key spot in the school day. (See Calkins 1986 for a sparkling discussion of how some teachers in New York have been working in this regard.)

But it is not just a matter of scheduling writing time and—"presto!" there is an addition to children's communicative competence. In classrooms where all children and the teacher are from the speech community whose language norms provide the basis for the school's language expectations, teachers still must learn how to elicit authentic writing and not some version of writing exercises. (See Edelsky 1986, Chapter Seven, for a presentation of the distinction between authentic writing and simulations of writing.) In classrooms where some students are not from the same speech community as each other, as the teacher, or as the school establishment, teachers not only have to learn how to refrain from substituting pretend-writing for writing; they also have to face different speech communities' varying written language norms.

In a ten-year ethnographic study of three speech communities in the Piedmont region of the United States, Heath (1983) found great diversity in conceptions of written language. Each community used writing for different purposes. Roadville residents wrote solely for transacting business or as an aid to memory; Trackton's residents treated print as a basis for group conversation or as an inspiration to oratory.

If speech communities vary in regards to norms for who says what to whom and how, so do they vary in who writes what to whom, how, and for what purposes. In some speech communities, women are not expected to read or write; in others, literacy problems (or even not reading or writing at all) are expected more often for males. In some communities certain "speech acts" are not written, only spoken (e.g., apologies or promises). There may be taboos on certain topics in written stories. A genre may have different syntactic or semantic choices in two communities. For example, letters to relatives in some U.S. Spanish speech communities end with elaborate syntax and flowery meanings (e.g., I like everything about this place, just as I like having you as my cousin). In many U.S. English speech communities, letters to relatives end with abbreviated phrases and casual, light meanings (Better quit now. Hope to hear from you soon). A genre may be common in one community, totally absent in another.

How can the teacher provide instruction in writing, trying to expand children's communicative competence, and still be sensitive to inter-speech community written language variation? As I said at the start, the potential difficulty stemming from *inter*community variation can be overcome with projects which rely on *intra*community variation (language variation according to the situation).

## Suggestions for Writing in Multi-Speech Community Classrooms

*Journals*

One written genre that seems to elicit positive responses from writers of many language backgrounds is the dialogue journal (Staton 1980; Staton, Shuy, Kreeft, and Reed 1987). Journals are something like a continuous letter exchange between student and teacher. Students write to the teacher; the teacher writes back but *never* red-pencils students' spelling or punctuation errors. The teacher may, however, deliberately use the same word or syntactic construction in replying, thus offering a model of the conventional form. The dialogue journal can provide students with a chance to complain to the teacher, to wonder with the teacher, to query the teacher. That is, the teacher can limit the assignment to a particular purpose, even a particular speech act. With such an assignment, both first- and second-language speakers of English grow in their ability to formulate full complaints or queries (Staton et al. 1987). More importantly, what that means is they have come to learn a style of thinking which goes along with those speech acts. Changing the purpose for writing from reporting to complaining, for example, entails a new relation to the addressee and different syntactic choices (e.g., He's always _____; I didn't like it when _____; whenever *X* then *Y*; etc.). Because the exchange is genuine, because the teacher responds and the response has a purpose other than evaluation, the teacher demonstrates how to perform other functions (e.g., defending against a complaint, offering to help, giving advice, etc.).

The predominant use of interactive dialogue journals does not, however, limit entries to one assigned purpose/speech act, like complaining. Instead, the purpose in many classrooms is for student and teacher to use journals to get to know each other better (Edelsky and Smith 1984). Children in those classrooms seem to begin their entries with the purpose of complying with an assignment. That is, the child's purpose at the beginning conflicts with the expectations for the genre of classroom journal. In those cases, the child is not writing at all, but is engaged in a writing exercise. How can a teacher prevent the journal from becoming pretend-writing? Often, the child's purpose becomes communicating with the teacher, if the teacher responds to the child's journal by disclosing something about herself, and requests that the child respond in turn to her. The journal then becomes authentic writing. A few children resist, either not wanting to know the teacher, not wanting to be known themselves, or not wanting to use writing as the resource for such a purpose. It is hard to know whether these cases have been the result of individual preferences or whether they can be tied to speech community variation in appropriate language behavior. It seems likely, however, that using journals for the purpose of developing an open-ended relationship between teacher and student is fraught with the potential for such clashes.

Substituting journals for diaries is another way journals are used in many classrooms. Here, the usual secrecy conditions of diaries are changed, and the teacher reads and replies to the entries. In this use of journals, the child is supposed to report events or thoughts or to work out problems, and the teacher comments on the child's entry but does little self-disclosing. There is no mention of using the journal for "getting to know each other" or for "letting each other know what we didn't get a chance to say in person." In addition to the problem of a possible speech community clash in norms for writing, the key problem with this use is that the genre is so contrived that children rarely buy into the purpose of confiding, and instead maintain the purpose of complying with an assignment. In that case, the activity becomes another writing exercise—pretend-writing.

If the activity is writing, and not some perfunctory or guarded simulation, journal writing is a supportive context for written language development, offering variation in purpose and genre to contrast with other genres. Topics can be suggested by either party; syntax and orthography can be demonstrated. Journals also offer a private avenue for interaction, something which might be very important to a second-language learner more embarrassed about speaking English than writing it under these conditions.

## Sophisticated Silliness

Language varies according to genre. Therefore, any shift to a different genre has the potential for stretching one's linguistic repertoire. Song lyrics, for instance, require different syntactic, graphic, and orthographic choices than does free verse. Language also varies according to tone or mood. Irony, for example, requires particular intonation contrasts; sarcasm violates expectations relating semantic choices to some aspect of the situation ("Quiet kid," says a bystander observing a tantrum).

There are contests that take advantage of knowledge of these kinds of variations. They make fun of genre expectations by exaggerating them. The Bulwer-Lytton Fiction Contest "challenges entrants to compose the worst possible opening sentence to a hypothetical novel" (Rice 1986). Named after the Victorian novelist who penned, "It was a dark and stormy night . . . ," its best worst openers have been published in a book of the same title, as well as in *Son of "It Was a Dark and Stormy Night"* (Rice 1986). An example of one ridiculously convoluted entry is:

> The hands of the little white porcelain clock, which had sat at her bedside since she was twelve years old and wildly in love with Baxton Heathley and which had been given to her by her Aunt Martha who had since died of a mysterious ailment in Peru while reportedly seeking information on the whereabouts of the famed black diamond which had belonged to her mother and her mother before her and so on down the line until it had disappeared during a hailstorm in Kansas where she was attending a convention of Astrologers Anonymous, crept slowly.

The contest's existence has created a new genre—Dark and Stormy Night-ers. Older students might enjoy working in groups to enter such contests or might establish local contests for similar spoofs (worst soap opera story line, worst song title, etc.).

A high school English teacher offered students a more risky opportunity to parody a genre. An ad in the back of a movie magazine proclaimed, "You too can become a song writer. Send us your song. We will tell you if you have talent." Spurred on by their teacher, groups of teenagers composed the most ridiculously bad lyrics they could, submitted them, and anxiously awaited their appraisal. The composing process was long, invested, and hilarious as the students talked on the phone to plan even better revisions for ever worse doggerel. The song company's responses, when read in relation to high schoolers' efforts, seemed even funnier than the lyrics. For example, next to the submission "Birdies fly in the sky/ birdie going bye-bye" the song company critic wrote, "rhyme scheme needs some work."

Writing such pieces requires careful attention to specific genre expectations, as well as devices for fulfilling them. If the tone of the group event for composing the entry as well as of the entry itself is humor, and the event seems to be fun, students may be hooked into this serious (but not solemn) attention.

## Making Communities' Knowledge the Curricular Focus

Wigginton (1972) made an Appalachian community's history the focus of investigation as well as a long-term publishing project; the *Foxfire* books and *Foxfire* magazine are both reference and symbol for that community and for the rest of the world. High school students in Heath's long study (1981) examined writing in the community (warranties, guarantees, regulations), and then rewrote much of it so that it was more usable by community members. In that same study (reported in Heath 1983), other children became ethnographers of the community's farming practices, translating the familiar community knowledge into unfamiliar academic means of display. These scholars and others have made some part of the community's knowledge the focus of inquiry. To work on the project, children had to interview, take notes, compile notes into drafts, write announcements, and so forth. That is, they wrote not to learn to write, but to learn something else. And in the process, they learned to write.

I want to carry this suggestion one step further. When students come from a variety of speech communities, variation in the language norms can itself be a curricular focus. Teacher and students together can study those norms and present their analyses to parent groups, the school board, other students, teachers' associations, or the general public. The analyses can be presented in newspaper articles or school newsletters or magazines. The object of study can be some aspect of communicative competence like naming practices (what are the rules for naming a new child; where is there leeway to these rules; are there differences in naming according to gender; who decides the name, and who must agree; can a name be changed, and if so, how; etc.), or compliments (what counts as a compliment; how do people respond to them; who gives them, to whom, where, about what). It could be something like how children and adults talk to each other.

It could also be the community's written language usage. Even young children can observe and record who writes in their home, in stores they go to, in churches, and so forth. They can find out when writing occurs, where, what it is that gets written. They can interview their own community members to find out what writing means to them (e.g., does writing make a message more or less believable, more or less reliable, a story more or less entertaining, etc.). Some key features of such research projects are:

1. The answers cannot be found in a textbook.

2. Students and teachers alike must collect raw data and wrestle with the problems of categorizing and interpreting the data.

3. The topics are down-homey familiar, yet unknown enough in their particulars so that they are likely to be enticing to students and to other community members.

4. Audiences are real (parents, school board, peers, etc.); to be effective and appropriate, messages to these different audiences have to vary in choice from the language subsystems.

5. The information will be used by others (even if it is used merely for interest value in a newspaper "filler" article); therefore, the students' work in collecting and analyzing the information has societal value.

6. Although at its start the project is done because the teacher presented and assigned it, it is likely to be taken over and "owned" by the students.

7. The projects are big enough, have enough parts, and extend over enough time so that students need to plan and record plans, make lists to remind themselves and others, solicit written permission from certain authorities, take notes, plan interview questions, draw up categories, log interim explanations and intriguing tidbits, etc. That is, the extent of the project inherently builds in varying situations for varying language use. Moreover, if the project becomes owned by the students, they will know what they want and need to do next; it will be their intent rather than teacher assignment which moves the project along.

8. Project work is divided among small groups. That means plans are made orally and in writing. Interviews are oral, noted in writing, notes talked about, categorized and analyzed in writing, interpreted orally, summed up in talk, spelled out in writing. That is, talking surrounds the writing; writing hones the talk. Such projects provide many contexts for one language mode to augment the other. Harste, Woodward, and Burke (1984), Gere and Abbott (1985), Kucer (1985), and others maintain that "language fine tunes language" (Kucer 1985), and that talk supports writing development and vice versa.

9. Everyone can participate and be an expert at some time. Because the projects are long and multidimensional, tasks can be differentially allocated. And because information sources are local and non-public, students with access to those sources can be

experts even if their beginning English language proficiency or their nonstandard dialect might otherwise relegate them to less-than-expert status during the language arts part of the daily schedule.

10. Mainstream norms are investigated as well as those of other speech communities. No group is singled out as "them" to be put under a microscope.

11. Because the teacher does not know the answers (Just who does give exactly what kind of compliments in your speech community? Are you sure?), the teacher has an opportunity to model learning, to demonstrate a genuine interest in finding out, to show different ways of handling data as he or she works with it.

There are some cautions here. Teachers must guard against re-acting to specifics discovered about different groups' language use as though these were "weird," whereas the teacher's norms were "sensible," nor should the variations be patronized as exotica. Most teachers will not need this warning, because, like most people, they will find it fascinating to develop a conscious understanding of rules of behavior they have unconsciously followed for years; teachers are as likely as students to be swept up in the excitement of learning more about themselves and their "folkways."

Projects like the one described here supply contextual variation within the project (varied purposes, varied audiences, varied genres) so that students get a chance to learn the effect of different language choices that might go along with those contextual variations. They do not do this through having students pretend to use the language, through engaging them in practice lessons, such as "writing" a letter of inquiry which is never mailed about something the student doesn't care about to a non-existent business, or "writing" reports supposedly informing an audience who knows more about the topic than the report writer. Rather, they get students to learn to handle language demands of different situations by actually putting them in those situations. Students' use of the language in the service of studying their own communities' ways results from having a teacher who sees variation as a curricular treasure; it results in giving those ways, those communities, and those students the respect they deserve.

## References

Brown, P., and S. Levinson. 1978. Universals in Language Usage: Politeness Phenomena. In *Questions and Politeness: Strategies in Social Interaction,* edited by E. Goody. New York: Cambridge University Press.

Calkins, L. 1983. *Lessons from a Child.* Exeter, N.H.: Heinemann.

———. 1986. *The Art of Teaching Writing.* Exeter, N.H.: Heinemann.

Dyson, A. 1982. Teachers and Young Children: Missed Connections in Teaching/Learning to Write. *Language Arts* 59 (7): 674–80.

Edelsky, C. 1986. *Writing in a Bilingual Program: Había una Vez.* Norwood, N.J.: Ablex.

Edelsky, C., and K. Smith. 1984. Is that Writing—or Are Those Marks Just a Figment of Your Curriculum? *Language Arts* 61 (1): 24–32.

Gere, A., and R. Abbott. 1985. Talking about Writing: The Language of Writing Groups. *Research in the Teaching of English* 19 (4): 362–85.

Goffman, E. 1959. *The Presentation of Self in Everyday Life.* Garden City, N.Y.: Doubleday.

Graves, D. 1983. *Writing: Teachers and Children at Work.* Exeter, N.H.: Heinemann.

Harste, J., V. Woodward, and C. Burke. 1984. *Language Stories and Literacy Lessons.* Portsmouth, N.H.: Heinemann.

Heath, S. B. 1981. Toward an Ethnohistory of Writing in American Education. In *Writing: The Nature, Development, and Teaching of Written Communication, Volume 1,* edited by M. Whiteman. Hillsdale, N.J.: Erlbaum.

———. 1983. *Ways with Words.* New York: Cambridge University Press.

Hymes, D. 1970. Bilingual Education: Linguistic vs. Sociolinguistic Bases. In *Bilingualism and Language Contact,* edited by J. Alatis, GURT No. 23. Washington, D.C.: Georgetown University Press.

———. 1972. Models of the Interaction of Language and Social Life. In *Directions in Sociolinguistics,* edited by J. Gumperz and D. Hymes. New York: Holt, Rinehart and Winston.

Kucer, S. 1985. The Making of Meaning: Reading and Writing as Parallel Processes. *Written Communication* 2 (3): 317–36.

Rice, S. 1986. *Son of "It Was a Dark and Stormy Night."* New York: Penguin.

Staton, J. 1980. Writing and Counseling: Using a Dialogue Journal. *Language Arts* 57 (5): 514–18.

Staton, J., R. Shuy, J. Kreeft, and L. Reed. 1987. *Dialogue Journal Communication: Classroom, Linguistic, Social and Cognitive Views.* Norwood, N.J.: Ablex.

Tannen, D. 1984. *Conversational Style.* Norwood, N.J.: Ablex.

Wigginton, E. 1972. *Foxfire.* New York: Doubleday. (*Foxfire* volumes 2–9 published 1973–1986.)

# 8 The Cognitive Academic Language Learning Approach

Anna Uhl Chamot
Second Language Learning, Washington, D.C.

J. Michael O'Malley
Georgetown University, Washington, D.C.

## Introduction

This chapter provides suggestions to elementary classroom teachers and secondary English and reading teachers on ways in which they can help their second-language students achieve greater success in content-area subjects. Mainstream teachers have an important role in furthering the education of ESL students in their classrooms, both in identifying and overcoming any difficulties these students may experience and in capitalizing on their background as a resource to other students. First, we will explain some of the reasons second-language students encounter academic difficulties related to both language and prior educational experiences. Then we will describe an instructional system designed to develop the academic language skills and learning strategies of these students in ESL classes, and show how many of the same techniques can be used by classroom teachers to further the academic development of their ESL students. Finally, we will present a lesson plan model that can be used to improve the academic competence of both first- and second-language speakers in a mainstream classroom.

## Background

When students speaking little or no English first enter school, they are usually placed in a language program to develop English skills for one or more years. Two general types of programs are available to these students: English-as-a-second-language (ESL) and bilingual programs. In ESL programs, students receive intensive instruction in

108

English-language skills for part of the day and spend the remainder in their regular classroom. In bilingual programs, students also receive ESL instruction, but the remainder of the day is spent in basic skills instruction in the native language. The rationale for bilingual programs is that skills such as reading and problem solving are transferable across languages; by providing instruction in a language that students can understand, greater progress may be achieved in the long run. Second-language students, whether in an ESL or a bilingual program, leave the program as soon as they demonstrate a level of proficiency in English that teachers and test performance indicate will allow them to function successfully in the all-English mainstream curriculum. Deciding exactly when a student has reached an adequate level of English proficiency is a difficulty faced in both ESL and bilingual programs. The most frequently used language proficiency tests tap social, interactive, and basic literacy skills, only a small portion of the total array of language skills required in academic subject areas.

Of the minority-language background students entering mainstream classrooms after a bilingual or ESL program, some will have already learned English and some basic skills well enough to make satisfactory progress in their schooling. But many of these students will still have problems learning in English and will encounter serious difficulties with the academic subjects. The record shows high dropout rates for such students (Bennett 1986; Duran 1983; O'Malley and Schmitt 1987), with the result that they are denied opportunities for participating successfully in our society.

Researchers have attributed many of the difficulties encountered by ESL students in mainstream classrooms to differences between the type of language used for ordinary social conversation and the type of language used for academic purposes, and the fact that these academic language skills take considerably longer to develop than social language skills (Collier 1987; Cummins 1983; Saville-Troike 1984). Cummins (1981) analyzed the school records of 1,200 immigrant minority-language students in Canada, and found that while most developed social interactive skills in English in about two years, five to seven years were needed before students were able to use academic language appropriate to their grade level.

A recent study confirmed Cummins's findings and provided additional information about the relationships between age of arrival and amount of previous education on school achievement by immigrant students in the United States. Collier (1987) examined the standardized achievement test scores of over 1,500 immigrant students who had been mainstreamed after completing an ESL program.

These students, with the exception of five- to seven-year-olds, had been at grade level in their native countries when they arrived in the United States of America. Collier found that immigrant students entering school between the ages of eight and eleven needed four to five years to reach an average score at the fiftieth percentile on nationally standardized tests of reading, language arts, science, and social studies. These eight- to eleven-year-olds needed the least time to become moderately successful in mainstream instruction, as evidenced by standardized test scores. Students entering school at ages five to seven without initial primary education in their native countries were less advanced academically than the older group. For these younger students, a period of five to eight years was needed to reach the same standardized test norms. At greatest academic risk were students who had arrived in the United States at age twelve or older. These middle and secondary school students were only at about the fortieth percentile on most tests after four to five years of instruction, which included both ESL and regular classroom instruction. Collier indicates that the heavy cognitive and academic language demands which students encounter in the secondary school make it difficult for them to catch up, and states that secondary students are most in need of content-area instruction (rather than only intensive English-language instruction).

Close collaboration between classroom and language specialist (ESL and bilingual) teachers is essential in meeting the educational needs of these students. Language development does not stop when students are not in ESL classes. All teachers need to work together to ensure that language skills are developed throughout the school day. Minority-language students may need more time than is usually provided for them to develop academic language skills in English in bilingual and ESL programs. In many cases, ESL students may also need help in how to learn academic content. Because of the attention devoted to language at the beginning level of ESL instruction, students may have had limited opportunities to develop effective learning strategies and study skills. Also, unless students have been in a content-based ESL class or maintained their subject matter development through instruction in their own languages, they can be expected to have significant gaps in content-area knowledge and skills. For these reasons, classroom teachers with students who are either in an ESL or bilingual program for part of the day or have recently exited from such a program need to continue to develop language skills and learning strategies in all areas of the curriculum. In the next section, we describe an instructional approach that can be used to teach language across the curriculum and to provide direct instruction in the use of learning strategies for all subjects.

## The Cognitive Academic Language Learning Approach

The Cognitive Academic Language Learning Approach (CALLA) is an instructional system designed to develop academic language skills in English for students in upper elementary and secondary schools. CALLA (pronounced *kala*) is intended for three types of ESL students (Chamot and O'Malley 1987):

- students who have developed social communicative skills through ESL or exposure to an English-speaking environment, but have not developed academic language skills appropriate to their grade level
- students exiting from bilingual programs who need assistance in transferring concepts and skills learned in their native language to English
- bilingual English-dominant students who are even less academically proficient in their native language than in English, and need to develop academic English language skills

The CALLA instructional system consists of three components: a content-based curriculum appropriate to the students' grade/developmental level; academic language development activities; and instruction and practice in using learning strategies. CALLA was originally designed as a transitional ESL program for students at intermediate and advanced levels of English proficiency, but the instructional techniques we advocate can be effectively used by mainstream teachers with second-language students in their rooms.

CALLA is based on theory, research, and practice. In this chapter, an overview of the theoretical model underlying CALLA is described first. Next, a discussion of the three components of CALLA and how each can be developed by the classroom teacher is presented. Finally, a lesson plan model focusing on the development of academic language skills and concepts in English is described.

### Theoretical Model

CALLA is based on a theory which suggests that language is a complex cognitive skill, similar in many respects to other complex cognitive skills (such as reading for comprehension, writing, and problem solving in mathematics). The theory indicates that learning a language is similar to learning any other complex cognitive skill; that is, learning a language has more in common with learning complex cognitive skills than it does with learning facts, isolated pieces of information, or even meaningful texts. Therefore, many of the techniques that classroom teachers use in teaching other complex skills will apply directly to teaching the ESL learner. In this section, we identify four aspects of complex cognitive skills, and then derive implications for teaching.

First, complex cognitive skills consist of procedures (Anderson 1985). These procedures are based on complex sequences or steps that learners begin to master gradually as they compile larger units of the skill. As in learning the procedures to perform a borrow and carry operation in mathematics, students may learn the procedures for a language skill such as regular and irregular pluralization.

Second, it takes a very long time to master complex cognitive skills. In language learning, the procedures are so complex, and the possibilities of combinations are so limitless, that achieving mastery level performance of the skill may easily take several years (Collier 1987; Cummins 1983; Saville-Troike 1984).

Third, any complex skill is best learned when the learner can try to perform complete sequences of the procedure, no matter how inexpertly, and receive cued feedback upon encountering difficulties (Gagné 1986). This is in contrast to learning a set of rules, rehearsing and repeating the rules until they are committed to memory, and then attempting to use the rules as a guide to performance. The best feedback in second-language acquisition is immediate and responds to the learner's intended meaning, rather than to any errors committed in the attempt to communicate. Feedback that is based on the success of meaningful communication may be provided by other students as well as by the teacher.

Fourth, it may be difficult to transfer a complex skill learned in one environment to another environment or to a different linguistic task. For example, ESL students may comprehend present progressive constructions (I am _____ing) quite well when they hear or read them, but still say "I am go" or "I going."

These aspects have implications for teaching. One implication is that second-language development may progress most effectively when learners can use the language on the type of materials for which they are expected to demonstrate mastery. This is why we recommend using authentic content-related materials in a content-based ESL classroom to prepare students for the same type of materials in a regular classroom. A second implication is that the learner needs to receive immediate feedback, and since the teacher cannot give every student immediate feedback on every utterance, the teacher should use peer tutoring in cooperative learning situations with students whose English proficiency is at varying levels. A third implication is that the teacher should make sure that all four language areas—writing, listening, speaking, reading—are included in every lesson and in every content area. This addresses, at least in part, the problem of transfer.

## The Three Components of CALLA

The three components of CALLA (grade-appropriate content, academic language development, and learning strategy instruction) are integrated into an instructional system which teaches ESL students how to use the language and learning strategies that they need for success in academic areas of the curriculum. Although CALLA was originally designed as a transitional ESL program, the educational principles of CALLA can be applied to mainstream classrooms with both native- and non-native-English-speaking students. This is because CALLA is based on research about how students learn both concepts and skills—whatever the language. Teaching students how to learn more efficiently by applying appropriate learning strategies and including language activities in all areas of the curriculum is, we believe, beneficial to all students, not just ESL students.

## The Content-based Curriculum

When CALLA is taught in an ESL program, the curriculum is carefully aligned with the all-English curriculum that students will eventually enter, so that practice is provided with a selection of the actual topics students will encounter in the mainstream classes. The intent is not to duplicate the mainstream curriculum, but to prepare the students to enter that curriculum, one subject at a time. We recommend that different subjects be phased in the following sequence: first science, then mathematics, then social studies, and finally, language arts (literature and composition, not ESL).

Why do we recommend moving the ESL student gradually into the curriculum? We recommend beginning with science because, by using a discovery approach to science, teachers can provide hands-on activities, which are so important for the ESL speaker. The next subject, mathematics, is highly abstract in the upper grades, and has more restricted language than science. The third subject, social studies, has heavy reading and writing demands as well as potentially unfamiliar cultural information. Language arts is introduced last because grade-appropriate literature and composition are often the most difficult for ESL students; not only is a high level of English required, but so is a shared background of cultural assumptions. In a CALLA classroom, content topics are carefully selected to represent both authentic topics at grade level and high priority topics within the curriculum. Classroom teachers can work closely with ESL and bilingual teachers, sharing their content objectives and major topics of study, so that common curricular objectives can be taught by both mainstream and language specialist teachers.

A common reaction to the less-than-fluent English of a student is to teach content from a lower grade level and to expect only lower-level cognitive skills, such as simple recall. CALLA demands the opposite. ESL students need to learn content that is appropriate to their developmental level and prior educational experience, and higher-level thinking skills are as much to be expected from them as from any student. Teachers should ask higher-order questions and evaluate responses on the basis of the ideas expressed, rather than on the correctness of English. Rather than watering down content for second-language students, teachers can make challenging content comprehensible by providing additional contextual support through demonstrations, visuals, and hands-on experiences. Also, teachers can help students apply learning strategies in order to understand and remember the content presented. Suggestions for doing this are presented later in this chapter.

Academic Language Development

In CALLA's second component, students practice using English as a tool for learning academic subject matter. These academic language skills may or may not have been developed in the first language, so students may either need instruction on how to transfer previously learned skills to English, or may need to learn academic language for the first time.

Why should academic language be particularly difficult for ESL students? There are two factors, according to Cummins (1982, 1983), that affect language comprehension: context and cognitive complexity. Language that is most comprehensible takes place in a here-and-now context that is rich in both nonverbal cues (such as concrete objects, visual aids, and gestures) and in opportunities to interact with people and things. For example, a child has a good chance of understanding the term *red ball* when she and a friend are playing with several toys and the friend points and asks her to "throw the red ball." Her chance of understanding this highly contextualized term is much less when she is asked to look at a workbook page with three circles, and is told that the one in the middle is a red ball.

The language of classrooms is sometimes called "decontextualized" because often the language does not refer to hands-on activities, but to ideas and events that are far removed from the immediate setting. Furthermore, the language of classrooms is often complex and requires manipulation of difficult concepts, especially in content areas. Thus, academic language is both decontextualized and high in cognitive complexity. The schooling process gradually develops in children the skills necessary to use this sort of academic language through the use of contextual supports for meaning in the early grades. But when ESL children enter mainstream classes at the upper elementary or secondary level, they may not be able to manipulate academic concepts in English in a decontextualized instructional setting.

ESL students can begin developing academic language skills in English through cognitively demanding activities in which comprehension is assisted by contextual support. Some of these activities include (Chamot and O'Malley 1987):

Developing an academic vocabulary in different content areas.

Understanding academic presentations accompanied by visuals and demonstrations.

Participating in hands-on science activities.

Using manipulatives to discuss and solve math word-problems.

Making models, maps, graphs, and charts in social studies.

Participating in academic discussions and making brief oral presentations.

Understanding written texts through discussion, demonstration, and visuals.

Using standard formats as supportive structures for writing simple reports in science and social studies.

Answering higher-level questions orally.

These and similar content-based language activities provide opportunities for ESL students to develop academic language proficiency in English while participating in mainstream classrooms. The language arts and English teacher can assist this development by including in their classes materials and concepts drawn from the content areas. For example, some reading exercises might include skimming a scientific article, scanning a mathematics word-problem, and taking notes on a chapter in a social studies textbook. Writing activities could include additional expository writing related to content areas, so that students learn how to organize a science laboratory report and how to do library research for a history paper.

Learning Strategy Instruction

The third and central component in CALLA is instruction in learning strategies. This is a cognitive approach to teaching that assists students by identifying and teaching conscious techniques that facilitate learning both language and content. We have four main reasons for advocating this sort of instruction (Chamot and O'Malley 1987):

1. Mentally active learners are better learners. Students who organize new information and consciously relate it to existing knowledge should have more cognitive linkages to assist comprehension and recall than do students who approach each new task as something to be memorized by rote learning.

2. Strategies can be taught. Students who are taught to use strategies and provided with sufficient practice in using them will learn more effectively than students who have had no experience with learning strategies.

3. Learning strategies transfer to new tasks. Once students have become accustomed to using learning strategies, they will use them on new tasks that are similar to the learning activities on which they were initially trained.

4. Academic language learning is more effective with learning strategies. Academic language learning among students of ESL is governed by some of the same principles that govern reading and problem solving among native English speakers.

Many older ESL students may have developed learning strategies attuned to educational experiences in their native countries. For example, in an educational system that places a high value on assimilation of facts, students might learn highly effective rote memorization strategies. Other strategies, however, are needed for integrative language tasks such as reading for information, explaining a process, or developing a report. Many students, whether proficient in English or not, need direct instruction and extensive practice in using learning strategies appropriate to different types of academic tasks. Teachers who have used CALLA in classes with both mainstream and ESL students report that instruction in learning strategies is as beneficial to native speakers of English as it is to students learning English as another language.

Teaching ESL students to use conscious learning strategies can accomplish three important goals: learning language, learning through language, and learning to learn. Studies that have taught English-speaking students to use learning strategies to improve their reading comprehension and their ability to solve problems in math and science have demonstrated that learning strategy instruction can be successful (Romberg and Carpenter 1986; Weinstein and Meyer 1986; White and Tisher 1986). In extending this research to second-language learners, we have concluded that learning strategies seems to be as effective for learning language as they are for learning in other areas. Good language learners use many different learning strategies, often in quite intricate ways, to help them understand and remember new information, whereas less effective learners have fewer strategies and apply them infrequently or inappropriately (O'Malley, Chamot, and Kupper, in press).

We have identified three major types of learning strategies used by students (O'Malley et al. 1985a):

> *Metacognitive strategies*, which involve executive processes in planning for learning, monitoring one's comprehension and production, and evaluating how well one has achieved a learning objective.
>
> *Cognitive strategies*, in which the learner interacts with the material to be learned by manipulating it mentally (as in making mental images, or elaborating on previously acquired concepts or skills) or physically (as in grouping items to be learned in meaningful categories, or taking notes on important information to be remembered).
>
> *Social-affective strategies*, in which the learner either interacts with another person in order to assist learning, as in cooperation or asking questions for clarification, or uses some kind of affective control to assist a learning task.

In studying learning strategies used in different contexts, we have come to the conclusion that a group of general learning strategies may be of particular use for ESL students who are learning both language and content (Chamot and O'Malley 1987). Figure 1 lists and defines this group of learning strategies.

Some of the learning strategies in Figure 1 are often thought of as study skills. Study skills describe overt behavior, such as taking

## Metacognitive Strategies

Advance Organization

Previewing the main ideas and concepts of the material to be learned, often by skimming the text for the organizing principle.

Organizational Planning

Planning the parts, sequence, main ideas, or language functions to be expressed orally or in writing.

Selective Attention

Deciding in advance to attend to specific aspects of input, often by scanning for key words, concepts, and/or linguistic markers.

Self-monitoring

Checking one's comprehension during listening or reading, or checking the accuracy and/or appropriateness of one's oral or written production while it is taking place.

Self-evaluation

Judging how well one has accomplished a learning activity after it has been completed.

## Cognitive Strategies

Resourcing

Using target-language reference materials such as dictionaries, encyclopedias, or textbooks.

Grouping

Classifying words, terminology, or concepts according to their attributes.

Note-taking

Writing down key words and concepts in abbreviated verbal, graphic, or numerical form during a listening or reading activity.

Summarizing

Making a mental or written summary of information gained through listening or reading.

Deduction/Induction

Applying rules to understand or produce the second language, or making up rules based on language analysis.

Imagery

Using visual images (either mental or actual) to understand and remember new information.

Auditory Representation

Playing back in one's mind the sound of a word, phrase, or longer language sequence.

Figure 1. Learning Strategy Definitions (Chamot and O'Malley 1987)

(*Figure 1 continued*)

| | |
|---|---|
| Elaboration | Relating new information to prior knowledge, relating different parts of new information to each other, or making meaningful personal associations to the new information. |
| Transfer | Using previous linguistic knowledge or prior skills to assist comprehension or production. |
| Inferencing | Using information in an oral or written text to guess meanings, predict outcomes, or complete missing parts. |

### Social-Affective Strategies

| | |
|---|---|
| Questioning for Clarification | Eliciting from a teacher or peer additional explanation, rephrasing, examples, or verification. |
| Cooperation | Working together with peers to solve a problem, pool information, check a learning task, model a language activity, or get feedback from an oral presentation. |
| Self-talk | Reducing anxiety by using mental techniques that make one feel competent to do the learning task. |

notes, writing summaries, or using reference materials, while learning strategies generally pertain to unobservable mental processes. Students need to learn study skills, the overt behavior associated with learning strategies, and they also need to learn to use non-observable strategies, such as monitoring for comprehension, elaboration of prior knowledge, and inferencing. Learning strategies can be defined, then, as how a person thinks and acts to complete a task.

A good way to initiate learning strategy instruction is to find out what strategies students are already using for different learning activities. Teachers can interview students about ways they approach specific classroom tasks and can also have students "think aloud" as they take turns working on a task. These two activities can help students become more aware of the mental processes they engage in when approaching and solving a problem, and can help teachers diagnose learning strategy needs. After identifying strategies that students are already using, teachers can use the strategy list in Figure 1 to select, model, and provide practice with additional strategies.

In summary, learning strategy instruction can play an important role in teaching both ESL and native-English-speaking students by showing them how to apply effective learning techniques to language and content learning.

## Planning a CALLA Lesson

In order to integrate the three components of CALLA into an instructional plan, we have developed a lesson plan model that incorporates learning strategy instruction, content-area topics, and language development activities. In this plan, learning strategy instruction is embedded into daily lessons so that it becomes an integral part of the regular class routine, rather than a supplementary activity. In this way, both second-language and proficient English-speaking students have opportunities to practice the strategies on actual lessons, and use of the strategies becomes part of the class requirements. At first, teachers show students how to use the strategies, often by modeling, and then continue to remind students to use them. Later, teachers remind students less frequently so that they can begin to use strategies independently. Discussion of learning strategies that different students find effective should be ongoing in a CALLA classroom.

CALLA lessons are useful for all students because all students can profit from the integration of language and content and the development of effective learning strategies.

CALLA lessons include both teacher-directed and learner-centered activities. Each CALLA lesson plan is divided into five phases. These are: preparation, presentation, practice, evaluation, and expansion activities. These brief descriptions of each phase indicate how content topics, academic language skills, and learning strategies can be developed in a CALLA lesson.

*Preparation.* In the preparation phase of the lesson, the teacher finds out what students already know about the concepts to be presented and practiced, what gaps in prior knowledge need to be addressed, and how students have been taught to approach a particular type of learning activity or content area. At the same time, students have the opportunity to remember and value their prior knowledge as they begin to connect it to the lesson topic. Another valuable aspect of this initial discussion is that students can share their different approaches to completing the task. In the preparation phase, the teacher should check essential vocabulary needed for the lesson and, if necessary, develop labels in English for concepts known in the native language.

The learning strategies commonly practiced in the preparation phase are advance organization (students preview the lesson) and elaboration (students recall relevant prior knowledge).

*Presentation.* In the presentation phase of the lesson, new information is presented and explained to students in English that is supported by contextual clues, such as demonstrations and visuals. Teachers need to make sure that ESL students are comprehending the new information so that they will be able to practice it accurately in the next phase of the lesson. The following suggestions can help the classroom teacher present information that is comprehensible to their ESL students as well as their native-English-speaking students.

- Monitor your own language for clarity, precision, pace, and word choice. When presenting key vocabulary and concepts, define, paraphrase, and give an example.

- Contextualize the language used during presentation of new information (either by the teacher, the text, or other information source) by using concrete objects, pictures, manipulatives, demonstration, miming.

- Use the chalkboard to provide visual backup to the information presented by writing key words and concepts, drawing graphs and charts, or graphically indicating relationships.

- Group students homogeneously for presentation of especially difficult or language-demanding information, and provide additional explanation and illustrations to ESL students.

- Group students heterogeneously for small-group cooperative learning in order to maximize interaction between students, and provide extra incentives for group performance.

- Maintain a supportive affective climate for ESL students by responding to intended meaning (even when expressed in inaccurate English), showing interest in and respect for students' home cultures, and involving ESL students in class activities with native-English-speaking students.

- Encourage ESL students to ask questions for clarification when they do not understand; model appropriate questions when necessary; and provide specific guidelines for classroom participation.

- Ask ESL students higher-level questions about the material presented rather than only factual recall questions.

Some of the learning strategies practiced in this phase are: selective attention (attending to or scanning for key ideas), self-monitoring (students check their degree of comprehension), inferencing (guessing meaning from context), note-taking, imagery (imagining descriptions or events presented), and questioning for clarification.

*Practice.* The practice phase of the lesson is learner-centered, as students engage in hands-on activities to practice the new information they were exposed to in the presentation phase, and the teacher now acts as facilitator. A variety of types of practice should be provided so that students can assimilate the new information and use it in different ways. Cooperative learning in heterogeneous teams is particularly effective during the practice phase, as students can work together in small groups to clarify their understanding of the information previously presented. ESL students can profit from working in small groups with native English speakers, who can serve both as language models and tutors. The learning strategies typically practiced in this phase of the CALLA lesson are: self-monitoring (students check their language production), organizational planning (planning how to develop an oral or written report or composition), resourcing (using reference materials), grouping (classifying concepts, events, terminology), summarizing, deduction, imagery (making sketches, diagrams, charts), auditory representation (mentally playing back information presented by the teacher), elaboration, inferencing, cooperation (working with peers), and questioning for clarification.

*Evaluation.* In the evaluation phase of the lesson, students check the level of their performance so that they can gain an understanding of what they have learned and any areas that need review. Evaluation activities can be individual, cooperative, or teacher-directed. Teachers can assess higher-level comprehension by focusing on the meaning of student answers rather than on their grammatical correctness. Learning strategies practiced in the evaluation phase of a CALLA lesson are: self-evaluation, elaboration, questioning for clarification, cooperation, and self-talk (assuring one's self of one's ability to accomplish the task).

*Expansion.* In the expansion phase of the lesson, students are given a variety of opportunities to think about the new concepts and skills they have learned, integrate them into their existing knowledge frameworks, make real-world applications, and continue to develop academic language. This phase also provides the opportunity to exercise higher-order thinking skills such as inferring new applications of a concept, analyzing the components of a learning activity, drawing parallels with other concepts, and evaluating the importance of a concept or new skill. Some expansion phase CALLA lessons ask students to interview family members about parallels in their native culture to topics presented in class. These home interviews will probably be conducted in the native language, but are then reported in class in English. By finding opportunities to include information about ESL students' cultural and linguistic background in class activities, classroom teachers not only assist in the development of positive self-concept but also provide native-English-speaking students with valuable multicultural experiences. In the expansion phase of a CALLA lesson, any combination of learning strategies appropriate to the activities can be practiced.

The CALLA lesson plan allows for flexibility and different types of activities. We recommend cooperative learning activities for part of each lesson because cooperation not only improves student performance, it also provides additional opportunities for students to use academic language skills for a learning task. The five phases of a CALLA lesson will vary in duration depending on the lesson topic and the extent of students' prior knowledge. The structure of a CALLA lesson helps ensure that students have many opportunities to practice learning strategies and to use academic language skills as they work on grade-appropriate content. Finally, CALLA lessons are organized to facilitate a learner-centered classroom in which all activities are designed to meet student needs and to help students become aware of themselves as mentally active and competent learners.

## Conclusion

We have described some of the major language-related difficulties that ESL students encounter in mainstream classrooms and have suggested ways in which classroom teachers can assist minority-language students to continue their English language development across the curriculum.

First and most important, we have suggested that classroom teachers need to collaborate closely with language specialist teachers in planning educational activities for ESL students. Classroom teachers can provide assistance to language specialist teachers by sharing with them the major curriculum objectives of the subject(s) they teach, so that these same objectives can be addressed in the ESL or bilingual program. Classroom teachers can also benefit from suggestions and ideas that language specialist teachers can provide on integrating language development activities in all areas of the curriculum. Finally, both mainstream and language specialist teachers need to work together to develop specific instruction on learning strategies for all students, with the ultimate aim of creating autonomous learners.

## References

Anderson, J. R. 1985. *Cognitive Psychology and Its Implications.* 2d ed. New York: W. H. Freeman.

Bennett, W. J. 1986. *The Condition of Bilingual Education in the Nation, 1986: A Report from the Secretary of Education to the President and the Congress.* Washington, D.C.: Department of Education.

Chamot, A. U., and J. M. O'Malley. 1987. The Cognitive Academic Language Learning Approach: A Bridge to the Mainstream. *TESOL Quarterly* 21 (2): 227–49.

Collier, V. P. 1987. Age and Rate of Acquisition of Cognitive-Academic Second Language Proficiency. Paper presented at the annual meeting of the American Education Research Association, Washington, D.C.

Cummins, J. 1981. The Role of Primary Language Development in Promoting Educational Success for Language Minority Students. In *Schooling and Language Minority Students: A Theoretical Framework.* Los Angeles: California State University, Evaluation, Dissemination, and Assessment Center.

————. 1983. Conceptual and Linguistic Foundations of Language Assessment. In *Issues of Language Assessment Volume II: Language Assessment and Curriculum Planning*, edited by S. S. Seidner. Wheaton, Md.: National Clearinghouse for Bilingual Education.

Duran, R. 1983. *Hispanics' Education and Background: Predictors of College Achievement.* New York: College Entrance Examination Board.

Gagné, E. D. 1986. *The Cognitive Psychology of School Learning.* Boston: Little, Brown.

O'Malley, J. M., A. U. Chamot, and L. Kupper. In press. Listening Comprehension Strategies in Second Language Acquisition. *Applied Linguistics*, vol. 10.

O'Malley, J. M., A. U. Chamot, G. Stewner-Manzanares, L. Kupper, and R. P. Russo. 1985a. Learning Strategies Used by Beginning and Intermediate ESL Students. *Language Learning* 35 (1): 21–40.

————. 1985b. Learning Strategy Applications with Students of English as a Second Language. *TESOL Quarterly* 19 (3): 557–84.

O'Malley, J. M., and C. Schmitt. 1987. *Academic Growth of High School Age Hispanic Students in the United States.* Washington, D.C.: Center for Education Statistics, U.S. Department of Education.

Romberg, R. T., and T. P. Carpenter. 1986. Research on Teaching and Learning Mathematics. In *Handbook of Research on Teaching*, 3d ed., edited by M. C. Wittrock. New York: Macmillan.

Saville-Troike, M. 1984. What Really Matters in Second Language Learning for Academic Achievement? *TESOL Quarterly* 18 (2): 199–219.

Weinstein, C. E., and R. E. Mayer. 1986. The Teaching of Learning Strategies. In *Handbook of Research on Teaching*, 3d ed., edited by M. C. Wittrock. New York: Macmillan.

White, R. T., and R. P. Tisher. 1986. Research on Natural Sciences. In *Handbook of Research on Teaching*, 3d ed., edited by M. C. Wittrock. New York: Macmillan.

# 9 A Road to Success for Language-minority High School Students

David Freeman and Yvonne S. Freeman
Fresno Pacific College, California

Emilia, Miguel, Feliciana, and David graduated from high school in June. The year before their parents, teachers, counselors, and even the students themselves had little hope that they would receive their diplomas with their classmates. A special summer program made the difference for them and many of their peers (Freeman, Freeman, and Gonzales 1987). This program was developed by teachers, consultants, and administrators working together to approach the teaching of content to secondary students in a way that would help language-minority students succeed in school. By examining how the program was set up, how the teachers were prepared, how the lessons were approached, and how the students came to view learning, we are able to draw some conclusions about how secondary teachers with no knowledge of their students' first language can help second-language students succeed in content-area classrooms.

The key elements of the program are indicated in Figure 1: the *who, what, when* and *where* set the scene, and the *how* describes the principles that the teachers applied to help these language-minority students reach their potential and discover that learning can be

| | |
|---|---|
| **Who:** | Students whose first language was not English. Students with low standardized test scores. Students who had failed at least three classes. Two content-area teachers hired by the district. Two ESL student teachers. |
| **What:** | Intensive summer classes in required United States history and biology courses. |
| **When and Where:** | Two three-week sessions of summer classes meeting from 7:00 a.m. to noon, in an urban school in Arizona. |
| **How:** | Teachers applied four learning principles. |

Figure 1. Key Elements of the Special Summer Program

worthwhile. We will discuss each of these key elements in some detail, because we think that what helped these teachers and students can also help other similar students in secondary content-area classrooms.

## Who: The People

### The Students

The forty-six students involved in the summer program had just finished their freshman or junior years of high school. The home language survey administered by the district indicated that their first language was either Spanish or Yaqui. However, the students had not had the benefit of instruction in their native language, and had been in mainstreamed classes during all of their schooling in the United States.

The minority status of the students was not the only criterion used to determine placement in the program. In addition, the participants had experienced little previous academic success. All had scored below the forty-first percentile on the California Achievement Test, and all had failed at least three courses during the previous school year. They were high-risk students. Such students often drop out of school when they reach the legal age to do so (Wong Fillmore 1986; Duran 1983). The classes, then, were made up of students who were identified by the district to be potential dropouts.

Emilia, Miguel, Feliciana, and David are representative of the group as a whole. They demonstrated oral proficiency in their second language, English. Although they spoke Spanish or Spanish and Yaqui, they had never received any schooling in either of these languages and had never developed academic skills in their first language. Therefore, instruction in their first languages—with the extensive vocabulary that would be necessary for the study of the science and social studies courses—did not seem appropriate, nor was it available through the school district. None of the four students appeared to have developed the literacy skills necessary for academic success in either their first language or in English. What they needed was a special kind of classroom instruction in English that differed from the traditional instruction they had experienced in school thus far.

### The Teachers

The two content-area teachers for the classes were regular classroom teachers with no previous experience in this type of program. Rob, the history teacher, teaches gifted classes during the regular school year and originally took the summer job because he wanted the extra salary. Ruben, the biology teacher, has taught science in regular and bilingual classrooms for several years. Ruben did not usually teach summer school, but took the job at the last minute when the teacher originally scheduled could not teach.

The two student teachers, Carrie and Sue, were completing their master of arts degrees at the local university and wanted their student teaching experience in a high school classroom. Though these ESL teachers were not experts in biology or history, they understood language acquisition theory and methods of teaching English as a second language.

**What: The Courses**

Two required courses were offered during the summer: biology and United States history. The courses were specifically designed to help academically troubled language-minority students succeed. The district administration, which fully supported these courses, insisted that the content be the same as during the regular year. The difference in these summer courses was the instructional approach of the teachers, which was supported by the student teachers and local university consultants. Staff from the university not only conferred with administrators, resource personnel, and teachers, but also with the school board itself so that approval for the program came from the district's main governing board.

Initially, Stephen Krashen made a presentation to the school board. He reviewed his theory of language acquisition (1981, 1985), emphasizing the need for comprehensible input. Once the board approved the plan, the university consultants came to the school for pre- and inservice meetings with the teachers, student teachers, district administrators, and resource people.

An important condition set by the board was that the materials and tests not be "simplified" and that the students be required to do the same work that students did during the regular school year. As a result, the challenge for all involved was to find ways to make the academic coursework "comprehensible input" to these students.

**When and Where: Time and Place**

The program was held in two three-week sessions. Classes met daily from 7:00 a.m. to noon during June and July. This, of course, meant that the coursework was intense, because it condensed a full year's course into six weeks of instruction. Daily attendance was mandatory since each day represented a week's work.

The classes were held in Arizona at an urban school site. The biology class and the United States history class were only two of the many classes held there that summer. Although these two classes were considered pilot classes by the district, other students at the school were not aware that these courses were anything more than regular summer "makeup" classes.

## How: Applying Principles

In the preservice training and during the time the classes were being taught, the consultants asked the teachers to apply four principles of learning that have been suggested at different times for first-language learners and second-language elementary school students (Goodman 1986b; Goodman and Goodman 1981; Harste, Woodward, and Burke 1984; Goodman, Goodman, and Flores 1984; Cazden 1986; Hudelson 1984, 1986; Rigg 1986; Urzúa 1986; Enright 1986; Enright and McCloskey 1985). During the preservice sessions the principles were discussed and sample lessons were demonstrated. As teachers and consultants worked together with students in the classroom, they used the principles as a base to help them reflect upon what was happening in the classroom.

The principles are:

1. Learning occurs most easily when language is kept whole.
2. Classes should be learner-centered and include activities that are meaningful and functional.
3. Learning takes place in social interaction that employs all four modes of language.
4. Learning requires that teachers have faith in learners.

We next describe each of these principles, and we give examples of how they were applied in the two content classes.

### Language Is Learned Best When Kept Whole

Researchers and theorists in first-language acquisition have argued that language learning is a gradual differentiation of wholes into parts, not a building up of parts into the whole (Vygotsky 1962; Smith 1973; Cochrane et al. 1984; Rich 1985; Goodman 1986b).

Often second-language students are given more drill and practice on isolated bits and pieces of language than native speakers of English are because it is assumed that whole, meaningful language is too difficult for them. But many second-language educators disagree. Allen (1986) points out, "The kinds of language arts experiences which support English-speaking children to develop and shape their skills in communicating in their native language are also the kinds of experiences that can support the LEP child as he or she takes on a new language" (61). Enright and McCloskey (1985) note, "Children learn language as a medium of communication rather than as a curriculum subject with sets of isolated topics, facts, or skills" (434).

In the summer program, the teachers were encouraged to apply the principle that learning takes place from whole to part in their content classrooms. Rather than having their students memorize bits and pieces of information about biology or history, the teachers began with whole concepts and let the details fall into place as students developed an understanding of the concepts.

For example, in the United States history class, Rob and Carrie began the unit on the American Revolution by asking students to talk about what *revolution* meant, why countries had revolutions, where there were revolutions right now, and finally, what they knew about the American Revolution. Students and teachers brought in current periodicals with articles about present-day revolutions. Carrie read the students a short story about the American Revolution to help make the characters and setting of the period come alive (Brozo and Tomlinson 1986). Students then read the social studies text, compared what they read with the information about revolutions they had already gathered, and worked in groups to decide what the major causes of the American Revolution were, what events and people were important to the outcome, and how the American Revolution could be compared to other revolutions discussed in class.

## Classes Should Be Learner-centered, with Meaningful, Functional Activities

The teachers in the summer program began by focusing on what the students already knew in order to build upon their strengths and interests. Often, content-area classes begin by finding out what the students don't know. These classes operate on the assumption that there is a great deal of information that students lack and that the teacher and textbooks will impart that information to the students. Teachers who hold this assumption view students as plants waiting passively to be fed and watered (Lindfors 1982). The teachers in this summer program were asked to view their students as explorers (Lindfors 1982), active learners who bring a great deal to the learning process and at the same time, draw from their environment as they develop new understandings.

The American Revolution unit which Rob and Carrie taught was designed to begin with what the students already knew and understood. The students shared their knowledge of revolutions in general and brought in information from newspapers and magazines about current revolutions. Then they compared these revolutions with what they read about the American Revolution. In this way, their understanding of the American Revolution was framed by their previous knowledge and experiences.

The unit on plants which Ruben and Sue taught also was designed to involve the students from the start. To begin the unit, students and teachers brought in fruits and vegetables from home for class. Then, the students worked in groups. They were given knives and told to study the fruits and vegetables at their tables and to record their discoveries. After a few minutes, students were making hypotheses about fruit parts, seeds, seed coverings, and plant growth. Feliciana, for example, noticed that onions are different from apples because onions have so many layers.

The following day students read the plant chapter in their textbooks. In the same groups, they compared what they read with what they had already discovered. Later in the unit they again used real fruits, vegetables, and plants as they drew and labeled plants, fruits, and seeds. As they worked with fruits and vegetables, conversations about what the students ate came up naturally. These conversations led to a lively discussion on nutrition. This evolved into a comparison of the kinds of fruits and vegetables that are traditionally present in typical American food and in the food the students eat at traditional family festivities. For example, in the American South, many people eat black-eyed peas on New Year's Day; on that day, tamales are usually served in the homes of these students.

By involving students actively and by making sure that the content of the units related personally to them, the teachers made the lessons meaningful and functional for their students. Student involvement extended from initial activities to final evaluation. Students wrote questions and answers about the content material that was covered. These questions were used by the students in cooperative groups to quiz each other on facts (Kagan 1986) and formed the basis of classroom quiz games. The teachers also made a point of including some of the student-generated questions on unit tests. In these ways, classes were learner-centered. All class activities involved students in the learning process from the beginning of the units to the end when they were evaluated.

## Language Is Learned in Social Interaction

Most of the activities in the classrooms involved pairs, small groups, or large groups. In fact, when students were left to work on their own, some did not enjoy it. David complained in his journal, "The thing I don't like is when we have to go off on our own and do our own notes."

First-language researchers (Halliday 1975; Wells 1985) have shown that language develops in social interaction. Second-language researchers and theorists also support group work for language-minority students (Long and Porter 1985; Enright and McCloskey 1985; Kagan 1986). When students work in groups they actually use more language, take greater risks, and help each other learn more.

In both the American Revolution unit and the plant unit, students worked together constantly. Students came up with ideas together, discussed concepts together, turned in joint projects at the end of the units, read and responded to textbooks together, wrote and answered questions about the content together, and even shared their journal writing with one another.

As the students worked together, they used all four modes of language—writing, listening, reading, and speaking. In many secondary classrooms, the role of the teacher is to talk while the students' role is to listen, read the textbook, and answer questions. The summer school teachers changed these traditional roles which both teachers and students usually take on. Students did much more of the talking as they shared what they knew, and read and discussed the class content materials together. As a result, students also listened to each other more as they worked together to understand the concepts they were studying.

Both the students and the teachers noticed the difference. Miguel pointed out that when he walked down the hall, other classrooms were quiet, with the students writing and reading alone at their desks, and the teachers sitting at their desks. "The only two classrooms where there is anything interesting going on are our United States history class and that biology class down the hall." Rob made a similar observation from the teacher's point of view:

> The first day I came in and, despite the inservice suggestions,
> I started lecturing as usual. I soon realized the students were

not listening and that my usual use of sarcasm to discipline and get their attention was not as effective as I had always assumed it was. Now that I have involved students and used group work, I will never again depend solely on lecture, textbooks, and tests to teach. Involvement in this summer program has changed my teaching with all students.

Social interaction extended beyond oral language activities to writing. Students wrote daily. They did not simply answer questions on tests or from their textbooks; instead, they kept daily journals that either their teachers or their peers responded to. In these journals, the students reacted to events that had happened in class or to the class content. They used the journals to ask questions, to express their opinions, and to work out ideas they were beginning to understand. Emilia, when studying the Civil War, asked, "Why didn't the first Constitution get rid of slavery?" Feliciana wrote about a brainstorming session, "I enjoyed when we got into a group today and how we thought of what to write on the board from what we could remember. It was long but fun . . ." David wrote about the seeds in fruits and vegetables, "The seeds were different sizes, but the size of the seeds doesn't match what grows . . ."

The history and biology classrooms became communities of learners using all four modes of language in social interaction to explore the content areas.

## Language Is Learned Best When Teachers Have Faith in Learners

The responses that Emilia, Feliciana, and David gave in their journals reflect an atmosphere in which they were willing to take risks. They felt free to ask questions, express opinions, and make hypotheses because they knew that their teachers and peers would accept what they said or wrote as something that was potentially valuable and worth considering. For many of the students in this summer program, this was the first time that they had been in a classroom where they were encouraged to take risks and supported when they ventured opinions.

At the preservice sessions, the consultants and the teachers talked about how classes usually start out. In many high school classes, the first day is spent going over course requirements and rules. The course begins with the teacher setting out her or his expectations: "In order to pass this course, you must . . ." or "Unless you do this and this and this, you will fail," or "In my course, I expect you to . . ." or "If you do this, the penalty will be . . ."

The teachers of these summer courses agreed to try another approach. They took the attitude that their students could succeed and that they *would* succeed. They started the first day by explaining that their course would be different. They stressed that everyone in the course was going to succeed, and that the teachers and students were going to work together to help each other succeed. From the first day, the teachers made it clear to students that they could do the work successfully and that there would be a support group to help them.

As teachers drew on students' background knowledge, encouraged them to express their opinions and ask questions, and allowed them to work together to discover answers, students gained confidence in themselves as thinkers and learners. In an atmosphere where the teachers made it clear that they had faith in their students, the students were able to revalue themselves as learners (Goodman 1986a). At the same time, they began to revalue the coursework and to see it as something worth doing. Because their teachers had faith in them as learners, the students developed faith in themselves that they could learn. This change in self-perception for these particular students was the most important result of the program, because the attitude that they could succeed in school carried over into the regular school year.

## Results

The results of the program were exciting. Students experienced success in school, some of them for the first time. They became actively involved in their own learning and succeeded. Even though he had seldom written to express himself before, Miguel wrote, without hesitation, his appreciation for the class and how it helped him:

> I think class helps me out a lot because in my other classes they never really explain and you people always explain everything that is about the subject that we are studying and i think that this class is pretty fun to be in because we have nice teachers for the class and if the teachers wasn't here to help us where would we be we all would be dumb. teachers help alot its seemed that this class i'm in i'm learning more then i learned last year and on the first test i took in here was the best test i have ever had and i thank you teachers for the help

Besides responding in their journals, students had an opportunity to evaluate the class by completing a questionnaire on their perceptions and attitudes (Figure 2).

It is significant that ninety-five percent of the students responding to the survey either strongly agreed (#5) or agreed a little (#4) that "working in groups helped me." Ninety percent agreed by marking #4 or #5 that they would like more classes conducted like this one, and seventy-three percent agreed they were ready for tests because

On a scale of 1–5, show how you feel about the items listed. Agree or disagree by checking (√) your responses as follows:

Check:  #5 if you *strongly agree*
   #4 if you *agree a little*
   #3 if you *are undecided*
   #2 if you *disagree a little*
   #1 if you *strongly disagree*

|  | 5 | 4 | 3 | 2 | 1 |
|---|---|---|---|---|---|
| 1. I was able to participate more in this class because of the way it was conducted. | 58% | 30% | 10% |  | 2% |
| 2. Working in groups helped me. | 70% | 25% | 5% |  |  |
| 3. I liked working in groups. | 62% | 25% | 10% | 3% |  |
| 4. The teacher(s) made an extra effort to help us understand the material and learn more. | 68% | 15% | 11% | 6% |  |
| 5. The class was presented in an interesting way. | 49% | 35% | 8% | 8% |  |
| 6. There were many different types of activities that benefited us. | 27% | 50% | 13% | 10% |  |
| 7. I was ready for the tests because we studied, discussed, and reviewed the material in class several different ways. | 48% | 25% | 5% | 12% | 10% |
| 8. I liked this class because I learned. | 55% | 35% | 8% | 2% |  |
| 9. I would like more classes conducted like this one. | 70% | 20% | 5% |  | 5% |
| 10. I got to know many of the students in class. | 60% | 26% | 7% | 7% |  |
| 11. I feel better about school because of the help I got in class. | 53% | 21% | 18% | 8% |  |
| 12. I learned some skills in this class that I can use in my other classes next year. | 43% | 47% | 10% |  |  |

Figure 2. Students' Perceptions and Attitudes

of the way the material was reviewed. Perhaps the most significant percentage for these students, who were considered potential drop-outs, was question eleven: seventy-four percent agreed with the statement "I feel better about school because of the help I got in class."

Student grades also reflected the students' feelings about school. All but two students in the two classes passed the course and those students failed because they did not fulfill strict attendance require-ments. Some students received an *A* or *B* for the first time since elementary school. One girl wrote: "This is the first class I've had since seventh grade that I passed a test without cheating." Students felt the classes helped them and that their time was well spent. Emilia sums up the attitude of many of the students in realistic terms:

> I think this class is not to bad, this is my first time in summer school, and I have began to like it. eventhough its kind of boring sitting in your seat for 5 hrs. but with the work we do it makes it alot easier to go threw the day. Working in groups is not to bad either because you get to meet outher classmates and it gives you an oppurtunity to see how much their interested in this class too, and it make work alot easier cause you can all work and help each other I feel that the time I will be here it will be worthwhile and I will be getting something out of it.

By working on whole concepts, drawing on student strengths and understandings, encouraging group interaction, and having faith in the learners themselves, teachers were able to help these students change their view of themselves as learners. The success of this program suggests that other schools with similar student populations might benefit from trying out and refining the techniques outlined here.

## References

Allen, V. G. 1986. Developing Contexts to Support Second Language Acquisition. *Language Arts* 63:61–66.

Brozo, W. G., and C. M. Tomlinson. 1986. Literature: The Key to Lively Content Courses. *The Reading Teacher* 40:288–93.

Cazden, C. 1986. ESL Teachers as Language Advocates for Children. In *Children and ESL: Integrating Perspectives*, edited by P. Rigg and D. S. Enright, 7–22. Washington, D.C.: TESOL.

Cochrane, O., D. Cochrane, S. Scalena, and E. Buchanan. 1984. *Reading, Writing, and Caring*. Winnipeg: Whole Language Consultants, Ltd.

Duran, R. P. 1983. *Hispanics' Education and Background*. New York: College Entrance Examination Board.

Enright, D. S. 1986. Use Everything You Have to Teach English: Providing Useful Input to Young Language Learners. In *Children and ESL: Integrating Perspectives*, edited by P. Rigg and D. S. Enright, 113–62. Washington, D.C.: TESOL.

Enright, D. S., and M. L. McCloskey. 1985. Yes, Talking! Organizing the Classroom to Promote Second Language Acquisition. *TESOL Quarterly* 19:431–54.

Freeman, D., Y. S. Freeman, and R. D. Gonzalez. 1987. Success for LEP Students: The Sunnyside Sheltered English Program. *TESOL Quarterly* 21:361–67.

Goodman, K. S. 1986a. Revaluing Readers and Reading. Occasional Paper no. 15, Program in Language and Literacy, College of Education. University of Arizona.

———. 1986b. *What's Whole in Whole Language?* Portsmouth, N.H.: Heinemann.

Goodman, K. S., and Y. Goodman. 1981. Twenty Questions about Teaching Language. *Educational Leadership* 38:437–42.

Goodman, K. S., Y. Goodman, and B. Flores. 1984. *Reading in the Bilingual Classroom*. Rosslyn, Va.: National Clearinghouse for Bilingual Education.

Halliday, M. A. K. 1975. *Learning How to Mean: Explorations in the Development of Language*. London: Edward Arnold.

Harste, J. C., V. A. Woodward, and C. L. Burke. 1984. *Language Stories and Literacy Lessons*. Portsmouth, N.H.: Heinemann.

Hudelson, S. 1984. Kan Yu Ret an Rayt en Ingles: Children Become Literate in English. *TESOL Quarterly* 18:221–38.

———. 1986. ESL Children's Writing: What We've Learned, What We're Learning. In *Children and ESL: Integrating Perspectives*, edited by P. Rigg and D. S. Enright, 23–54. Washington, D.C.: TESOL.

Kagan, S. 1986. Cooperative Learning and Sociocultural Factors in Schooling. In *Beyond Language: Social and Cultural Factors in Schooling Language Minority Students*, 231–298. Los Angeles: University of California, Evaluation, Dissemination, and Assessment Center.

Krashen, S. 1981. Bilingual Education and Second Language Acquisition Theory. In *Schooling and Language Minority Students: A Theoretical Framework*, 51–79. Los Angeles: University of California, Evaluation, Dissemination, and Assessment Center.

———. 1985. *Inquiries and Insights*. Hayward, Calif.: Alemany Press.

Lindfors, J. 1982. Exploring in and through Language. In *On TESOL '82*, edited by M. Clarke and J. Handscombe, 143–156. Washington, D.C.: TESOL.

Long, M. H., and P. A. Porter. 1985. Group Work, Interlanguage Talk, and Second Language Acquisition. *TESOL Quarterly* 19:207–28.

Rich, S. 1985. Whole Language—A Quick Checklist. *Whole Language Newsletter* 3:5–6.

Rigg, P. 1986. Reading and ESL: Learning from Kids. In *Children and ESL: Integrating Perspectives*, edited by P. Rigg and D. S. Enright, 55–92. Washington, D.C.: TESOL.

Smith, F. 1973. *Psycholinguistics and Reading.* New York: Holt, Rinehart and Winston.

Urzúa, C. 1986. A Children's Story. In *Children and ESL: Integrating Perspectives*, edited by P. Rigg and D. S. Enright, 93–112. Washington, D.C.: TESOL.

Vygotsky, L. S. 1962. *Thought and Language.* Edited and translated by W. Hanfmann and G. Vakar. Cambridge: MIT Press.

Wong Fillmore, L. 1986. Teaching Bilingual Learners. In *Handbook of Research on Teaching*, edited by M. C. Wittrock, 648–70. New York: Macmillan.

Wells, C. G. 1986. *The Meaning Makers.* Portsmouth, N.H.: Heinemann.

# 10 "Teaching" English through Content-area Activities

Sarah Hudelson
Arizona State University, Tempe

If we were to visit any number of elementary and secondary school classrooms, probably the dominant way students would be asked to learn would be through using textbooks. Students would be asked to open their books, to read out loud or silently, to answer oral or written questions, and perhaps later, to be tested on the content. While significant numbers of educators would question this practice for any student, this way of approaching content and texts is particularly inappropriate for students whose native language is not English.

However, ESL students are in the classrooms, and the expectation is that they should receive the school's curricula in the content areas. So what are teachers to do? One way of addressing this problem is to use content-area material as a vehicle for language development (Cantoni-Harvey 1987; Chamot and O'Malley 1987; Terdy 1987). The specific approach proposed here involves examining the content-area objectives that school districts and/or state departments of education create, and then beginning the teaching of content there, rather than with the textbook. But looking at content-area objectives themselves is not enough. What is necessary is the combining of content-area goals with some specific principles of learning in general, and language learning in particular, in order to move from the objectives to sets of activities that will provide meaningful learning experiences for students still developing as English users. The following principles, based on personal interpretations of some recent literature on first- and second-language development, may be used as a starting point for developing learning activities from content-area objectives:

## Principles

1. Students learn both content and language by being active, by doing things, by participating in activities directly related to

specific content, and by using both oral and written language to carry out these activities. Language develops holistically, not in parts. Language develops through use, not through isolated practice (Lindfors 1987). This is true in both a native and a second language.

2. Students learn both content and language by interacting with others as they carry out activities. These "others" may be both other students (peers) and adults who provide input and authentic reasons to communicate (Enright and McCloskey 1985; Krashen 1982; Lindfors 1987; Urzúa 1980). This is true in both a native and a second language.

3. All of the language processes are interrelated, and students become more able language users when they make use of all the processes in classroom activities, when they are asked to use both oral and written language in varied ways and for varied purposes, and when they see the connections between experiences and oral and written language (Allen 1986; Goodman 1987; Hudelson 1984; Rigg and Enright 1986). This is true in both a native and a second language.

4. Students learn to read by interacting with whole, authentic texts (by reading), and they learn to write by creating whole, authentic texts (by writing), by having others react to what they have created, by revising their pieces, and by using their reading knowledge to help them write like readers. The acquisition of written language is a holistic process, as is the acquisition of oral language. Literacy is acquired through use, not through practice of isolated skills (Goodman 1987; Harste, Woodward, and Burke 1984; Smith 1982). This is true in both a native and a second language.

5. Reading comprehension is facilitated by having prior knowledge of the topic of the text (Barnitz 1985; Rigg 1986). Background knowledge may be activated or developed through classroom activities that involve all of the language processes, including reading from a variety of sources other than the textbook. This is true in both a native and a second language.

## Applications: Instead of the Text

Beginning with those principles, the rest of this chapter will illustrate ways that they may be applied to specific content objectives in the development of classroom activities. The objectives used have been developed by Dade County Public Schools, Florida, in the areas of math, science, health, and social studies.

*Objective: Children will understand family roles and division of labor within the family.* This is a primary-level social studies objective. In the Florida state-adopted social studies texts, children would be expected to read an informational selection, accompanied by pictures, that would talk about the jobs various members of the family are responsible for. They would also read a short piece about a mother going back to work outside the home, and the children feeling that the mother doesn't have time for them anymore. Our concern is the provision of activities for ESL children that will enable them to meet the content-area objective while using English to do so, but in ways that are more sensible than simply being exposed to the text material. What kinds of activities might be organized?

An initial activity might be a chart to fill out that would involve the children answering such questions as: In your family, who cooks the food? In your family, who washes the clothes? In your family, who cleans the furniture? In your family, who buys the groceries? The students would be divided into small groups. Each child would first fill out the chart individually, after which the groups would meet to compare their answers and come up with a group summary of responses to each question. Putting the students into groups means that they can help each other with reading and answering the questions. The group chart assignment will also mean that the children will have to talk to each other about what they have done individually. After the groups have had a chance to share and organize their data, the class would come back together and complete a whole-class chart.

The whole-class charting activity might be followed by a learning log activity. In a learning log, children use writing as a way of reflecting on content they have studied. In this case, children would respond in their learning logs to the following questions: What did you learn about your own family from doing this activity? What did you learn about the families of others in this class?

In addition to these activities, several books or stories that reflect the theme of family interdependence would be shared with the children during storytime and made available for the children to read on their own. Some examples of such titles are: *The Little Red Hen*, Aesop's *The Grasshopper and the Ants*, *Cinderella*, and Lois Lenski's *Family Small*. The stories would also provide an opportunity for groups of children to create a skit or play to share with others. Another activity based on the content and concepts would involve dividing the children into groups, giving them two or three different family situations, and asking the groups to take the roles of family members and act out what the family would do in each situation. All of these activities, spread out over several days or weeks, would give the children the opportunity to use English in both oral and written forms, in varied ways, as they came to understand the concept of family roles.

## Applications: Making the Text Readable

The activities used demonstrate clearly that it is not necessary or even advisable to be limited to the textbook in terms of content teaching and ESL learners. Content objectives may be achieved by using a variety of materials and activities. But if teachers either choose or feel compelled to use the textbook, a variety of activities could be undertaken to provide the children with necessary background experiences and language that should make their reading of the text successful. When the children do see the text, it is critical to begin their reading with a prereading activity that asks students to list what they already know about the topic, in this case, what they already know about family roles. An alternative would be to construct a semantic map or web of what the children already know about family roles. After what they already know has been listed or mapped, children would read the selection and then compare what they listed to what was actually in the selection. After reading, it is logical to ask, "What else did you learn about family roles from what you just read?" This means that the variety of activities just detailed here may be used as alternatives to the text, or they may be used as background builders to the text. In either case, it is important for the students to spend time working together with a content focus, including reading and writing for various purposes.

## Applications: Mathematics Example

Let's look at another objective, this time from mathematics. An intermediate and junior high math objective in Dade County is the following: *Students will determine probability, meaning equally likely or not equally likely events.* For many learners, the concept of probability might be most understandable if it were considered initially in a nonmathematical way by dealing with the idea of chance in people's daily lives. *Chance* refers to the idea that something might or might not occur. It could happen, but maybe it won't. Here, for example, are some questions that students might be put into groups to answer: "Who will win the city championship in football (or any sport) this year? Will all the members of our class be in school tomorrow? How many members of our class will have perfect math papers this week? Will you see a Toyota car on your way home from school this afternoon?" Students would consider these questions and come up with answers (their best guesses). After students have reported what their groups decided, the teacher could conclude that all of these were chance events, giving students the specific vocabulary for the concept that they have been investigating.

Having demonstrated the concept of chance, students could then begin to consider the concept of probability. In groups once again, students could deal with statements such as: "Which is more likely or more probable, that one of the students or that the teacher will be absent from school tomorrow? Which is more likely, that you will have pizza for breakfast or that you will have pizza for lunch? Which is more likely, that you will go swimming in the summer or in the winter?"

Students might also work in groups to come up with answers to such statements as: "Is it more likely than not that you can find the sum of 324 and 465? In Phoenix, Arizona, in July, is it more likely than not that the sun will be shining at noon?" Then groups could respond to similar statements by categorizing them as certain/uncertain/impossible. Sample statements: "I will use my brain sometime this week. My dog can write his name in Spanish. All new cars will use water instead of gasoline for fuel. We will see the sun tomorrow. I will sleep eight hours on Tuesday night. I will not sleep at all this week." Activities such as these will give students the opportunity to experiment with chance and probability in their own lives, to use their collective experiences and language abilities to consider the statements, and to develop an experiential understanding of probability to which the term *probability* may then be affixed by the teacher. First the concept, then the label.

Following these nonmathematical activities, the mathematical side of probability should be developed. In groups once more, students would solve a variety of probability problems by carrying out sets of written directions that would ask them to do such things as: Toss a coin into the air a certain number of times (twenty, for example) and record whether it lands heads or tails; toss a die a certain number of times and note whether the number of dots on the top face is even or odd; toss a die a certain number of times and note what numbers come up. Small-group charts would be shared with the rest of the class and used to construct entire-class charts.

As the learners solve these kinds of problems and struggle with answers to some of the questions, the learning logs would be a logical vehicle to use for enabling learners to consider what they were learning about probability.

For teachers interested in extending the ideas of chance and probability into other contexts and written material, an amusing book like Remy Charlip's *Fortunately, Unfortunately* could be used, both for a light change of pace and as a possible model for student creation of chance and probability stories. In this book a series of chance occurrences, one after the other, keeps the main character going from something good happening to something bad happening. Students could create their own fortunately/unfortunately, good luck/bad luck sequences which would utilize various chance happenings. All of these activities would serve as background and language builders that should ensure greater success with the probability problems in the mathematics textbooks.

### Applications: Science/Health Example

Another way to approach the task of combining language and content is to group together a set of related objectives, such as the following set of intermediate science/health objectives: *Children will define the basic food groups, will recognize and understand cultural differences in foods eaten, will define what is needed to stay healthy, will evaluate specific foods and diets in terms of how healthy they are.* What kinds of activities could be organized to help students achieve these objectives?

As an initial activity, children could be asked to keep a record or log of all the food that they eat over a certain period of time (for one or two days). These logs would be kept individually and then brought to school. In school students in groups would share their logs with the goal of determining which foods they all have eaten and which foods they have eaten are unique to them or to their ethnic or cultural group. After small groups have listed the foods eaten, a class list would be developed. Then small groups would work again to put the foods eaten into categories. How would the students categorize the foods they eat? Which foods would they put together, and why? After the groups have reached consensus about food groups (an activity that requires children to use language informatively and persuasively with each other), they might consult their textbooks or other written sources, including informational books, food group posters, etc., to compare their categories to those of nutritionists.

Another activity would involve children in using information about food groups to create their own menus. Using newspaper ads, students would be asked to come up with menus for certain meals. They could put together both menus reflecting what they would eat if they had a choice and menus reflecting well-balanced meals. In many areas ethnic grocery stores advertise their food specials in city and neighborhood newspapers and flyers, so advertising could be chosen that reflects cultural differences in what people eat. Mathematics could be added to the activity if students received a certain amount of money with which they would need to buy groceries for a certain number of meals for a certain number of people. A requirement could be that the meals are well-balanced in terms of representing the basic food groups. Again the text or other written material on the food groups, as well as newspaper advertisements, could be consulted to determine what foods could be used to represent certain groups and how many servings of which were recommended each day.

Still another way to examine foods would be a study of the nutritional elements in certain kinds of packaged foods, such as breakfast cereals. Students could be asked to bring in cereal boxes and then to compare the nutritional elements of their favorite cereals. As an extension, groups of students could create their own breakfast cereals, including name, package design, ingredients, and nutritional elements of the cereal that they created. In addition to the box and nutritional elements, students could create an advertisement for the cereal they had created, and they could try to sell their cereals to the others in the class. The advertising activity also demonstrates that an intermediate social studies/economics objective—understanding advertising as a way of persuading—could be incorporated into the teacher's plans. The students could pitch their cereal and others could vote on which cereal they would most like to eat.

It should be obvious by now that students have used talking, reading, and writing for a variety of purposes. From the point of view of reading, a wide variety of informational reading materials has been utilized. Additionally, reading material such as cookbooks created for children could be used by the students as they consider menus they would like to create. Fun books, such as *Strega Nona* by Tomie de Paola could be shared. *Strega Nona* is the tale of a witch and her magical pasta pot, a pot that runs out of control when Strega Nona leaves Big Anthony alone in her house. De Paola's wonderful wordless picture book *Pancakes for Breakfast* could be used by children to create their own written stories to share with others. Informational books such as those on vitamins and junk foods could be used by the children as sources of information about nutritional elements.

From the point of view of writing, children could create their own recipe books or bring in favorite recipes from home. Cooking could be carried out in the classroom, and taste tests performed to see which ethnic foods students preferred. Learning logs could be utilized as students considered what they had learned about nutrition. And all of these literacy activities necessarily involve students in talking with one another to accomplish various tasks. All of these are examples of the kinds of integrative language activities advocated as crucial to the language and cognitive growth of ESL students.

## Applications: Social Studies Example

Let's look now at content-area objectives from one more perspective, that of objectives which sometimes are divided into content objectives and process or skills objectives. Many of these objectives appear, albeit with some variation, at several educational levels. As an example, at both elementary and secondary school levels, social studies objectives in Dade County deal both with the content of immigration as a factor in United States history and with such "skills" or process objectives as timeline and map construction and interpretation. Both kinds of objectives could be joined together and activities developed that would be of interest and relevance and that would provide for necessary skill development. In terms of ESL, some of the same objectives could be used successfully with different age groups of second-language learners. From the point of view of language development, this kind of recycling of objectives would give students more opportunities to use content-focused language. What might change would be not so much the activities or interactive processes, as the sophistication of the students' products and some of the written materials utilized.

Looking at content objectives in the area of immigration, intermediate group objectives state that students will be able to explain that the people of the United States are immigrants linked to the rest of the world through their immigrant heritages, and that students will be able to tell how their own immigrant heritages link them to the rest of the world. (Obviously, this curriculum is not drawn from states like New Mexico or Arizona, both of which have large populations of ESL speakers whose ancestors preceded English speakers by many, many years.) At senior high level, the expectation is that students will be able to describe the role of immigration in the growth of this country, list chronologically and describe the waves of immigration to this country, and describe the contributions of various immigrant groups to the United States. An examination of the "skills" objectives reveals that students at both levels are expected to be able to use maps of various kinds, identify items on maps, and construct and interpret timelines.

In terms of activities that might enable students to meet these objectives, the most logical place to begin the study of immigration is with something that may be in the students' experiences: their own immigration to this country. One of the things that many students know or can find out about is information about their own families. So an initial assignment could be to ask students to find out where their ancestors came from, when they came to this country, why they came here, and any other important facts in their family's history that they would like to share. Students who didn't have the information on a firsthand basis might interview one or more family members in order to come up with what they needed to share. This might mean that the interview would be conducted in a language other than English, but the sharing in class would be in English. After the students had collected information about their families, they would divide into groups to share what they had learned and to create group charts about group members' ancestry and reasons for coming to this country. Group sharing with the class would result in a whole-class chart that would reflect the heritages of all the class. This should mean that everyone in class would be able to participate, whether their families have been in this country for five years or a hundred years or more.

A *caveat* should be issued here. The purpose of this activity is not to determine who may be here on an undocumented basis. Care must be taken in the use of this activity, so that families do not get the impression that the school is about to turn them in to INS. Also, some refugee students may have suffered such trauma in escaping their native land, perhaps watching members of their families be killed, that they do not feel comfortable with this assignment. The sensitive teacher may decide to explore the possibility of this activity before assigning it.

After a class chart has been developed, maps would be used to locate the countries of the students' ancestors. Countries of origin would be highlighted, as well as routes drawn to the countries. In addition, maps that focus on political changes, economic conditions, and geographic realities as factors in immigration could be used and interpreted.

From the initial activity based at least partially on the students' own experiences, several other projects could be undertaken. The teacher might share the history of his or her family's arrival in this country with the class and demonstrate the use of a timeline as one way of visualizing the chronology of one family coming to this country. The teacher's model could prove useful to students as they created their own individual timelines.

Instead of individual projects, students could be asked to investigate a variety of immigrant groups to this country, different sets of students taking different groups. As a part of a report that each set would prepare for the rest of the class, students would construct timelines illustrating their immigrant group's history and contributions made by the group to this country over the years. As they prepare their reports, students will make use of a variety of written sources, books, encyclopediae, news articles, magazines, maps, atlases, films and filmstrips, television programs, interview data, etc., which the teacher will help them choose and utilize based on what they can handle. Involved in this report-writing will be sharing of information, creating initial drafts, sharing what has been written, and revising and editing.

For a slightly less ambitious project, the teacher might take the text information on immigration and carry out a jigsaw activity by asking students in groups to read different parts of the material and to report to each other. Because each group will report on information that the others have not read, there will be an authentic reason for listening. At the conclusion of the jigsaw activities, students would create a class bulletin board about immigration. For some students, it would be interesting and important to raise issues such as: "Did everyone who came to this country come of their own accord? If not, how were the experiences different?" This would give students the opportunity to compare the concept of immigration, which many would see as voluntary, to the history of slavery in this country.

Report-writing for the purpose of different groups sharing information that they have learned already has been mentioned as one kind of writing students could do. What other kinds of writing could be carried out in terms of the objectives stated? Certainly learning logs could be used, as students were asked on a regular basis to consider what they had learned. Another meaningful writing project would be the construction of student autobiographies, with special emphasis given to each student's immigrant experience, whether this experience took place recently or several generations ago. As with the report projects, the creation of autobiographies could take several days or weeks to complete and the processes of drafting, sharing, receiving reactions, and revising should be utilized, from the point of view of expanding students' language abilities. In all of these activities, the processes students are engaged in should be viewed as at least as important as the final products.

In the examples given so far, little or no mention has been made of utilization of the arts, such as music, dance, and drama. Obviously these could be included here (and in other content areas). Songs such as Neil Diamond's "Coming to America" could be considered in terms of the message the song provides. Music from various countries and its influence in this country could be seen as part of the immigrant heritage and contribution. So could dance. The possibilities are many. From a set of objectives many weeks' interesting and meaningful work, for both teachers and students, may be developed.

### Summary

These, then, are some examples of one way of approaching the issue of combining language and content learning in classes, including ESL learners. This chapter has tried to illustrate both that important school content may be viewed as a vehicle for language development, and that language is crucial to students as the major way they have of demonstrating their knowledge of content. The perspective taken is that language and content learning do not mean isolated skills and drill work. The aim of the activities presented has not been to assure that students get the correct answers to questions at the end of the chapter. The perspective presented is not that of the transmission classroom, in which the teacher doles out knowledge or facts (content of some kind), and the students give it back. The aim of considering the objectives is not even that of "covering" all of the objectives in any content area, just so the claim can be made that the students "did" the material. All of the biases or perspectives just stated apply to native English speakers as well as to those developing a second language.

Rather, the major concern is that learners, whether they be ESL students or native speakers of the language, grapple with content-area concepts and information, and that they use language: to share what they know, to work through what they're learning; to ask questions about what they want to know; and to seek answers to their questions both from other people and from varying sources of material. This concern is realized in the activity-based approach delineated in the previous pages. From my perspective, this kind of approach does the following: (1) It provides students with the opportunity to use English in both oral and written forms, for varied purposes. That is, the approach demonstrates to students what English is for. (2) It adds to students' background of experiences, experiences that should help them as they cope with regular classrooms. (3) It adds to students' knowledge of and abilities to deal with English, because of the variety of things learners do and because of the ways they use language to do these things. (4) It demonstrates to students that learning can be fun, exciting, and challenging, and that we believe that our content learning does not mean isolated skills and drills work. I believe that we owe our students, and ourselves, no less.

## References

Allen, V. G. 1986. Developing Contexts to Support Second Language Acquisition. *Language Arts* 63:61–66.

Barnitz, J. 1985. *Reading Development of Nonnative Speakers of English*. Orlando, Fla.: Harcourt, Brace, Jovanovich, and the Center for Applied Linguistics.

Cantoni-Harvey, G. 1987. *Teaching ESL in the Content Areas*. Reading, Mass.: Addison-Wesley.

Chamot, A. U., and J. M. O'Malley. 1987. The Cognitive Academic Language Learning Approach: A Bridge to the Mainstream. *TESOL Quarterly* 21:227–50.

Enright, D. S., and M. L. McCloskey. 1985. Yes, Talking!: Organizing the Classroom to Promote Second Language Acquisition. *TESOL Quarterly* 19:431–53.

Goodman, K. 1987. *What's Whole in Whole Language?* Portsmouth, N.H.: Heinemann.

Harste, J., V. Woodward, and C. Burke. 1984. *Language Stories and Literacy Lessons*. Portsmouth, N.H.: Heinemann.

Hudelson, S. 1984. Kan Yu Ret an Rayt en Ingles: Children Become Literate in English as a Second Language. *TESOL Quarterly* 18:221–38.

Krashen, S. 1982. *Principles and Practices in Second Language Acquisition*. New York: Pergamon.

Lindfors, J. 1987. *Children's Language and Learning*. 2d ed. Englewood Cliffs, N.J.: Prentice-Hall.

Rigg, P. 1986. Reading and ESL: Learning from Kids. In *Children and ESL: Integrating Perspectives*, edited by P. Rigg and D. S. Enright, 55–91. Washington, D.C.: TESOL.

Rigg, P., and D. S. Enright. 1986. *Children and ESL: Integrating Perspectives*. Washington, D.C.: TESOL.

Smith, F. 1982. *Writing and the Writer*. New York: Holt, Rinehart and Winston.

Terdy, D. 1987. *Content Area ESL: Social Studies*. Palatine, Ill.: Linmore.

Urzúa, C. 1980. A Language Learning Environment for All Children. *Language Arts* 57:38–44.

# Editors

**Virginia Garibaldi Allen** has taught French as well as English. Her experience as a second-language learner and teacher has given her both knowledge of and a sympathy for the struggling language learner. A professor at The Ohio State University for several years, Allen has been both teacher-educator and researcher, publishing articles and books on language arts and on English as a second language. She directed two major programs at OSU, one preparing bilingual teachers and another preparing mainstream teachers who would have some ESL students. Allen is co-author of *Language Arts: An Integrated Approach*. Active in both the National Council of Teachers of English and TESOL, she currently chairs the NCTE-TESOL Liaison Committee.

**Pat Rigg** has a small consulting firm, American Language and Literacy, in Tucson, Arizona. Before establishing her consulting business, Rigg for many years taught ESL to adults from around the world, both in and out of university settings. She has taught teachers, mainstream as well as specialists in reading and in ESL, and trained community volunteers in schools with a few ESL students. Rigg has a long-time interest in both first- and second-language literacy, as her publications indicate. She is active in both NCTE and TESOL, and is now associate chair of the NCTE-TESOL Liaison Committee.

# Contributors

**Anna Uhl Chamot** is adjunct professor at Georgetown University and works at Second Language Learning as well. A researcher in language learning strategies, Chamot co-developed the Cognitive Academic Language Learning Approach with J. Michael O'Malley. She conducts teacher training based on this model and is currently implementing CALLA in the Arlington, Virginia, ESL program. Chamot's many articles have appeared in various journals and in collected works; she has also published content-area textbooks for ESL students.

**Carole Edelsky,** professor of curriculum and instruction at Arizona State University in Tempe, has written extensively about language, especially language variation. "What It Means to Talk Like a Lady" is the title of an article she wrote after researching male and female uses of language in faculty meetings. She and Sarah Hudelson wrote "Learning a Second Language When You're Not the Underdog" after they had visited bilingual classrooms and observed just how "bilingual" those classes were. Edelsky's book, *Writing in a Bilingual Classroom: Había una Vez* is a model of sociolinguistic research at the same time that it offers specific examples of educational assumptions, beliefs, and practices that promote or hinder written communication.

**Elizabeth A. Franklin,** now at the Center for Teaching and Learning in the University of North Dakota, Grand Forks, has a great deal of experience with Spanish-speaking youngsters, both in and out of the migrant stream. Bilingual in Spanish and English herself, Franklin has taught Hispanic children in schoolrooms, in Head Start, and in community-based summer programs.

**David Freeman** and **Yvonne S. Freeman** have taught English as a foreign language in Colombia and Mexico, and have taught English as a second language in the United States to students of different ages. Both presently teach at Fresno Pacific College in Fresno, California, where they co-direct the language development program. They have centered their work around a whole language approach, and both have published on this topic. Yvonne Freeman also has published articles on bilingual literacy from a holistic perspective. Her dissertation on Spanish basals was recognized as outstanding in 1988 by the National Association of Bilingual Education (NABE).

**Jean Handscombe** is coordinator for English as a second language/dialect for the North York Board of Education, a large multiethnic school district

155

in Toronto, where one out of four students K–12 is learning English as another language. She has traveled widely within North America and beyond, visiting ESL classrooms and talking with teachers. She has been both classroom teacher and researcher; her current administrative responsibilities of designing, delivering, and evaluating programs for literally thousands of students have given her unmatched breadth and depth of experience in ESL education. Handscombe has spoken and written extensively for both learners and teachers of ESL. In 1985 she was elected president of International TESOL.

**Sarah Hudelson** is presently associate professor in the Division of Curriculum and Instruction at Arizona State University in Tempe. She has served as a VISTA volunteer in south Texas with Hispanics living far below the poverty level; she also has worked as a university professor (Arizona State University, Florida International University, University of Miami), preparing graduate and undergraduate students to teach in bilingual and second-language settings. Hudelson has written widely, both curriculum materials for elementary students and scholarly articles in such journals as *TESOL Quarterly* and *Language Arts*. Her "Kan Yu Ret an Rayt en Ingles?" has become required reading in any class preparing teachers for one or more REAL students.

**Judith Wells Lindfors** is a professor in the Department of Curriculum and Instruction at the University of Texas at Austin. In addition to many articles, she has written the widely used textbook *Children's Language and Learning*, which was awarded the first Mina Shaughnessy Medal for best book by the Modern Language Association. Lindfors's special research interests include dialogue journals and children's questioning. She has used dialogue journals to teach English with students in South Africa and soon will undertake a similar project in India. She also is active in NCTE.

**J. Michael O'Malley** is director of the Evaluation Assistance Center (EAC) East at Georgetown University. He was trained as a research psychologist and has conducted studies in early childhood education as well as second-language acquisition. His most recent interests are in the applications of research on learning strategies to content-based instruction in English as another language. O'Malley and Anna Uhl Chamot have worked together for several years as educators and researchers.

**Carole Urzúa** has experience as a teacher in multicultural classrooms, a consultant, a teacher-educator, and as a researcher. Now at the University of the Pacific in Stockton, California, Urzúa teaches an overload of classes, researches in a whole language program in a nearby Riverside City School, assists her local Multiple Resource Center, and actively participates in TESOL, CATESOL, and the National Council of Teachers of English.